IF I
FORGET

BY **STEVEN
LEVENSON**

★

★

DRAMATISTS
PLAY SERVICE
INC.

2

For Whitney, always

IF I FORGET was originally produced in New York City by Round-
about Theatre Company (Todd Haimes, Artistic Director; Harold
Wolpert, Managing Director; Julia C. Levy, Executive Director;
Sydney Beers, General Manager) at the Harold and Miriam Stein-
berg Center for Theatre / Laura Pels Theatre on February 22, 2017.
It was directed by Daniel Sullivan, the set designer was Derek
McLane, the costume designer was Jess Goldstein, the lighting
designer was Kenneth Posner, the original music and sound design
was by Dan Moses Schreier, and the production stage manager was
Kevin Bertolacci. The cast was as follows:

LOU FISCHER .... Larry Bryggman
HOLLY FISCHER .... Kate Walsh
MICHAEL FISCHER .... Jeremy Shamos
SHARON FISCHER .... Maria Dizzia
ELLEN MANNING .... Tasha Lawrence
HOWARD KILBERG .... Gary Wilmes
JOEY OREN .... Seth Michael Steinberg

ACKNOWLEDGMENTS

Special thanks to David Berlin, Evan Cabnet, Jim Carnahan, Carrie Gardner, Robyn Goodman, Stacey Mindich, Daniel Sullivan, and Stephen Willems; to my family, for remembering; to John Buzzetti, for never doubting; to Todd Haimes, for his trust in me; to Jill Rafson, for her unstinting support of, and unwavering faith in this play; and finally, to Astrid, for being.

CHARACTERS

LOU FISCHER, 75

HOLLY FISCHER, 48, Lou's daughter

MICHAEL FISCHER, 45, Lou's son

SHARON FISCHER, 39, Lou's daughter

ELLEN MANNING, 43, Michael's wife

HOWARD KILBERG, 51, Holly's husband, Joey's stepfather

JOEY OREN, 16, Holly's son

SETTING

An old two-story, peeling paint white Colonial on a quiet residential street in Tenleytown, a white, upper-middle-class neighborhood in Northwest, Washington, D.C.

After the end of the twentieth century.

NOTE

A forward slash (/) indicates a point of overlapping dialogue.

If I forget thee, O Jerusalem,
let my right hand forget her cunning.
If I do not remember thee,
let my tongue cleave to the roof of my mouth...

O daughter of Babylon, who art to be destroyed:
happy shall he be, that rewardeth thee as thou hast served us.

Happy shall he be, that taketh and dasheth
thy little ones against the stones.

—Psalm 137

IF I FORGET

ACT ONE:
July 29, 2000

One.

A hazy, humid Saturday afternoon in July.
Outside, the dry buzzing of cicadas mingles with the sput-
tering cough of Metro buses and the rattle of air conditioners
in rotting wooden window frames.
Inside, it is climate controlled and cool.
The guest room.
Miscellaneous home medical equipment has been pushed
into a corner in a half-hearted attempt to hide it: a fold-up
wheelchair, a rollator, a metal cart carrying an oxygen tank,
a dozen unopened boxes of cotton balls, latex gloves, and
gauze sponges.
Prescription bottles are scattered on bookshelves, bureaus,
and a bedside table.
Ellen sits on the bed, speaking on a clunky Nokia cell phone.
Michael hovers nearby, anxious.

ELLEN. *(Into phone.)* Great.

  Beat.

Great.

MICHAEL. *(Impatient.)* What is so great?

  Pause.

ELLEN. *(Into phone.)* Great.

MICHAEL. Oh my God.

ELLEN. *(To Michael.)* She says it's completely safe. / She feels completely safe.

MICHAEL. / Well, that's incorrect. She's incorrect. I'm sorry, but.

ELLEN. *(Into phone.)* Because he's worried about you, honey…

MICHAEL. Is she watching the news?

ELLEN. *(Into phone.)* He says, if you saw the news here…

MICHAEL. Tell her to turn on the news.

ELLEN. *(Into phone.)* We don't want you to be scared, honey. / We're just concerned that it's a very volatile situation.

MICHAEL. / Of course we want her to be scared. How can she not be scared? The entire peace process collapsed three days ago…

ELLEN. *(Into phone.)* The peace process is very bad right now, honey.

MICHAEL. The peace process is *over.*

ELLEN. *(Into phone.)* The peace process is over.

MICHAEL. Oslo, the entire Oslo framework, is out the window.

ELLEN. *(To Michael.)* They have security with them twenty-four hours a day.

MICHAEL. Obviously, they have security. They should have security. / That's a given.

ELLEN. *(To Michael.)* / She says, the Birthright people, they don't let them visit anywhere that isn't a hundred percent safe.

MICHAEL. Where are they going tomorrow?

ELLEN. *(Into phone.)* Honey, where are you going tomorrow? *(Listening.)* The Wailing Wall?

MICHAEL. Excuse me?

ELLEN. *(Into phone.)* You should / be excited.

MICHAEL. / She's not doing that. Tell her, she's not going there, Ellen.

ELLEN. Dad's so excited for you to go there, he's jumping up and down. *(Listening.)* Everyone wishes you were here, too, honey, but we're so happy you're having such a good time.

MICHAEL. I'm not happy. Don't tell her I'm happy. I'm very unhappy.

   Ellen looks at Michael, as she listens.

ELLEN. It does feel a little bit strange being here. It's very…it feels very quiet. Without Grandma.

MICHAEL. Let me talk to her.

ELLEN. Do you want to say hi to Dad before…? Just a quick…?

Ellen listens for a moment.

MICHAEL. Can you give me the phone?

ELLEN. Well, we have the cell phone with us, in case anything, if you need to get us for anything.

MICHAEL. You're not going to give me the phone?

ELLEN. Love you, too. Bye, sweetheart.

Ellen hangs up.

She's going to call tomorrow night, when they check into the next hotel.

MICHAEL. She didn't want to talk to me?

ELLEN. I think she heard everything you wanted to say, Michael.

MICHAEL. Well, good.

ELLEN. And she was running out the door. Her friends were going to leave without her. They're doing a moonlight tour of Jerusalem.

MICHAEL. Perfect.

ELLEN. She could be spending this whole trip sitting in the hotel room by herself, OK? She's going out with people, she's doing all the activities…

MICHAEL. I guess, I just still don't really understand why we had to send our daughter to Israel in the most—the worst time to be in the Middle East / in the last twenty-five years.

ELLEN. / I did not, we did not "send" her anywhere. She's nineteen years old, she can make her own decisions.

MICHAEL. Well, except this was a decision, you did happen to encourage this particular decision.

ELLEN. Her doctor told us this would be the best thing for her, socializing with other, meeting people her own age…

MICHAEL. That's called an internship. That's a summer job at an ice cream parlor. It's not a ten-day bus ride through a war zone.

ELLEN. It is not a war zone.

MICHAEL. Not yet.

ELLEN. It means a lot to her, to be there, which frankly I think is not the worst thing in the world for a teenager to be interested in learning about her heritage.

MICHAEL. OK…

ELLEN. And you, being the Jewish parent here, I'd think you would maybe appreciate that.

MICHAEL. "Heritage" is actually, that's actually a very problematic concept, first of all.

ELLEN. Can we just—she's having a good time, thank God. Can we please try to just be happy that she's happy? For a second?

MICHAEL. Is she sleeping?

> *Ellen says nothing.*

Is she?

ELLEN. Yes, Michael, she is.

MICHAEL. You asked her that?

ELLEN. I didn't need to ask her that. I trust her to tell us if there's a problem.

MICHAEL. So she's eating? She's definitely, she's taking her medication / and…?

ELLEN. / I would have heard it in her voice if something was going on.

MICHAEL. That hasn't, historically, that hasn't always been the case.

ELLEN. *(Putting an end to the conversation.)* I think maybe right now you're upset about other things, Michael, OK? And you're putting all of that negative energy onto Abby…

MICHAEL. What other things?

> *Beat.*

What other things?

ELLEN. It's completely normal to feel / like—

MICHAEL. / I feel fine. I'm fine.

> *Beat.*

ELLEN. It's good that we're here. It means a lot to your dad to have you.

MICHAEL. Did he say that?

ELLEN. I could tell.

Michael nods, skeptical.

Why don't you go spend some time with him? Before everyone else gets here…

MICHAEL. I'm only halfway through the galleys.

ELLEN. It's his birthday.

MICHAEL. His birthday's Tuesday.

ELLEN. The two of you have a lot to talk about…

MICHAEL. I need to send the galleys back by Monday.

She gives him a look.

I have a deadline, Ellen.

ELLEN. Don't do this to me.

MICHAEL. Do what?

ELLEN. What you always do when we're at your parents' house. Lock yourself in this room, pretending you have work to do, and I'm stranded downstairs, trying to entertain your family.

MICHAEL. I do not always do that.

She looks at him.

I have occasionally done that.

They smile.

ELLEN. It is quiet, though. Isn't it?

MICHAEL. I didn't notice.

Beat.

ELLEN. When I told Abby, when I said, Dad wishes that you were leaving Israel and coming home. You know what she said?

Michael shakes his head.

She said, "I already am home."

Long pause.

MICHAEL. Huh.

Two.

The dining room.
A long wooden table.
Behind, an aging breakfront, filled with various heirlooms: wedding china, dulled brass candleholders, silver kiddush cups, sundry crystal stemware, and a scattering of sepia photographs.
Ellen sits with Holly.

HOLLY. She still hasn't called you?

ELLEN. I wish she would.

Howard enters, carrying two cups of coffee.

HOLLY. *(To Howard.)* Are you hearing this? It's been a year and she can't pick up a telephone?

HOWARD. I heard.

HOLLY. Every time I talk to her, I say, I must have said it a hundred thousand times—Howard, what do I say every time I talk to Jennifer?

HOWARD. Call / your aunt and uncle.

HOLLY. / I say, call Michael and Ellen. You live in the same city.

ELLEN. Well, and we would love to see her, show her the new place…

HOLLY. Oh my God, the new apartment. That's right. How is it? I need pictures. Where are my pictures?

ELLEN. We can send you pictures.

HOLLY. Is it safe? Do you feel safe?

ELLEN. In Park Slope?

HOLLY. I thought Michael said Brooklyn.

ELLEN. It is Brooklyn. It's a neighborhood in Brooklyn.

HOLLY. And that's safe?

ELLEN. It's very safe.

HOWARD. Better value, too, I bet. Brooklyn.

ELLEN. Oh, well, Manhattan wasn't even, we could never afford that.

14

HOLLY. I couldn't believe it when Michael told me you two were buying. I didn't think you would ever buy.

ELLEN. Well, it just felt like the right time. With Michael's career and Abby away at school…

HOWARD. Welcome to the wonderful world of homeownership.

ELLEN. Well, any time Jennifer wants to come over, we would be thrilled to have her.

HOLLY. She is so wrapped up in herself—one year at Tisch and she already, she thinks she's Helen Hunt.

ELLEN. She's liking it?

HOLLY. What's not to like? They play games. They sing songs. They cry. We're paying forty thousand dollars a year for Montessori school.

ELLEN. I'm sure it's a great experience…

HOLLY. What about Abby? How's Middlebury? What a phenomenal school that is.

ELLEN. *(Hesitant.)* You know, she really…the classes are terrific. She loves her classes.

HOLLY. Of course she does.

ELLEN. Socially it's still, I think it's been a little bit of an adjustment for her.

HOLLY. Oh no.

ELLEN. Well, no, just in terms of, she doesn't have a million friends yet or…

HOLLY. Oh no.

ELLEN. She's just, you know, we've been struggling with the same things with her since third grade…

HOLLY. The eating?

ELLEN. She's had issues with…you know, body image and…

HOLLY. Eating?

ELLEN. College, I think, it really exacerbated certain things. Being away from home for the first time maybe?

HOLLY. Absolutely. That's not easy.

ELLEN. She was in the hospital for a week in November. I don't know if you...

HOLLY. *(Nods.)* Sharon told me.

HOWARD. Oh my God.

HOLLY. Awful.

HOWARD. I didn't know that.

HOLLY. And she is such a beautiful girl, is the irony, isn't it?

ELLEN. She's doing better now. Much better. Second semester, she really started getting into the groove, I think, finally. Knock on wood.

    She does.

She actually started, she's gotten very involved with Hillel, which has been great.

HOWARD. Great.

HOLLY. Fabulous.

ELLEN. Yeah, she really, she started going to the Shabbat dinners, the holiday services...

HOLLY. Fabulous idea.

ELLEN. No, I know, she got very excited about learning more about Judaism, about the culture and history... It's been very...I think it's been really great for her. To have something she's so passionate about.

HOLLY. She's a good girl.

    Long, awkward pause.

ELLEN. How's Joey? He's been doing OK?

HOWARD.	HOLLY. *(Sunny.)*
He was suspended for two weeks.	He's doing great.

    Beat.

HOLLY. *(Changing the subject.)* Where the hell is Michael? We've been sitting here for twenty minutes.

ELLEN. He is upstairs. Working.

HOLLY. I think he's a workaholic. Do you know that?

ELLEN. Oh he's, it's non-stop.

HOLLY. It's like Howard. Howard is like that.

HOWARD. It's been a busy year.

ELLEN. Well, Michael's teaching three classes in the fall, and then on top of that his new book is coming out in a few months, which is what's making him really, he's obsessing over it. Every detail.

HOWARD. I didn't know Mike was writing a book.

HOLLY. The last time I tried to read something of Michael's, I couldn't understand anything he was talking about. It's so convoluted, the way he writes.

ELLEN. Well, the new book is actually, this one is a lot less academic. Which, we're hoping it's more accessible than his usual writing. Sells more copies. Which is, you know, *any* copies.

HOLLY. How's your job? Do you still love it?

ELLEN. "Love" is a pretty strong word... There are times when it's, I mean, when you feel like you're really making a difference...

HOLLY. I couldn't do what you do if you paid me a million dollars.

ELLEN. Well, it's important that children have advocates. Even if it isn't always pleasant.

HOWARD. I have a buddy, his sister was a social worker out in Anacostia, in the housing projects there. The things she was doing with those people...I mean, heroic.

ELLEN. I'm sure.

HOWARD. Yeah. She ended up, she killed herself actually.

> *Joey enters.*
> *He wears baggy jeans and Timberland yellow boots, and holds an empty, oversized can of Arizona iced tea.*

HOLLY. Look who's here.

JOEY. Were you talking about me? I heard my name.

HOLLY. You heard wrong. Say hi to your Aunt Ellen.

JOEY. Hi Aunt Ellen.

ELLEN. Hello.

HOLLY. Pull your pants up. No one wants to see your underwear.

> *Joey hikes up his pants.*

JOEY. Can I have another iced tea? I'm thirsty.

HOLLY. *(To Ellen.)* All the boys at his school now, this is what they do. Look at this one. Pants hanging at his butt. He thinks it's attractive.

JOEY. Can I have another iced tea now?

HOLLY. You just had one.

JOEY. I'm thirsty though. My mouth is like completely dried up.

HOLLY. You can drink water. You don't need more sugar.

JOEY. I don't like the water here. It tastes bad. Grandpa doesn't have a filter.

HOLLY. Where is Grandpa? I thought you were watching the baseball game together.

JOEY. He fell asleep.

HOWARD. Uh-oh. You must have worn him out, Joey.

JOEY. *(To Ellen.)* Is Abby coming today?

HOLLY. Aw. He loves his cousin.

ELLEN. Abby is actually in Israel right now.

JOEY. On Birthright?

ELLEN. You know about Birthright?

JOEY. One of my friend's cousins did it.

ELLEN. Oh great.

JOEY. He got blowjobs from all the girls on the trip.

ELLEN. Oh.

HOLLY. Hey. Is that how we talk?

JOEY. He did, though.

ELLEN. We're hoping Abby's trip is a little less exciting.

HOLLY. He doesn't know what he's talking about.

JOEY. How much do you want to bet?

HOLLY. Enough.

JOEY. Howard, can I please have an iced tea? I'm so thirsty.

HOLLY. What did I just say? What did I just tell you?

JOEY. I'm like *dying* of thirst.

HOWARD. I'm going to defer to Mom on this one.

JOEY. This is so unfair.

HOLLY. Get out of here, Joey. If you're going to just stand there, hocking about the iced tea, goodbye.

>*Joey walks off.*

JOEY. *(Mutters.)* Asshole.

HOLLY. What did you say?

JOEY. I didn't say anything.

HOLLY. You better start acting like a gentleman right now.

JOEY. I am acting like a gentleman.

HOLLY. Do you hear me? *Right* now.

JOEY. I'm sorry.

HOLLY. Go. Do something else. I don't want to see you right now.

JOEY. I said I'm sorry. / Jesus fucking Christ, Mom.

HOLLY. / Go. Goodbye. Goodbye.

>*Joey leaves.*
>*Beat.*

ELLEN. He is so grown up.

HOLLY. *(To Howard.)* You're just going to let him talk to me that way?

HOWARD. You dealt with it. You were dealing with it.

HOLLY. You're his father. He needs to hear from you.

HOWARD. *(Under his breath.)* Stepfather.

HOLLY. What was that?

HOWARD. Stepfather, I said. I'm his stepfather.

HOLLY. And what is the significance of telling me that?

>*Michael enters.*

HOWARD. Mike.

MICHAEL. I am so sorry.

HOLLY. Mikey.

>*Hug.*

ELLEN. Where were you?

HOLLY. We've been sitting here for forty-five minutes.

MICHAEL. I got stuck on, there was a work call that I forgot I needed to take.

ELLEN. I thought you were coming right down.

MICHAEL. I know.

HOWARD. Hey Mike. How are you, buddy?

 Handshake.

MICHAEL. *(To Ellen.)* It was one of my advisees. I'm sorry.

ELLEN. It's a Saturday.

MICHAEL. No, I know. He wanted to hash out the details for the conference we're putting together with Students for Nader.

HOLLY. Oh my God, don't tell me you're voting for that asshole, Michael. Please don't tell me that.

MICHAEL. I'm the faculty advisor for the group.

HOLLY. You are such a jackass, Michael. That's throwing your vote away. You want Bush to win?

ELLEN. Thank you. That's exactly what I keep saying.

MICHAEL. And Al Gore is not throwing your vote away? Corporate lackey Al Gore?

HOWARD. I was a McCain guy, so…

ELLEN. *(To Michael.)* How are you going to feel when Bush becomes the next president?

MICHAEL. I'm going to feel like there's no difference between four years of Bush and four years of Gore.

HOLLY. What a jackass.

 Michael holds up the chunky cell phone.

MICHAEL. Did you bring the plug from the car? The battery's running low.

ELLEN. Just turn it off.

HOLLY. Is that a cell phone? He has a cell phone?

MICHAEL. I'm not turning it off. If Abby needs us…

ELLEN. She's not going to call tonight. It's late there.

MICHAEL. Well, unless there's an emergency.

ELLEN. God forbid.

HOLLY. What are you, a heart surgeon, you need a cell phone?

ELLEN. It's a family phone.

MICHAEL. It's convenient.

HOWARD. I'm dying to get one.

HOLLY. You already have a car phone.

HOWARD. But this is for when you're not in the car.

HOLLY. You don't need that, Howard.

HOWARD. It's like Mike said. It's for emergencies.

HOLLY. You don't have emergencies.

MICHAEL. We should get the plug.

ELLEN. Can you sit with us for five minutes please?

    Michael hears the desperation in her voice, accedes.

MICHAEL. Of course.

HOLLY. Tell me more about Abby. How's her trip? She's having a good time?

ELLEN. She's having a great time.

HOWARD. How's the news coming out of there?

MICHAEL. Troubling.

ELLEN. There is no news. Nothing's happening. It's all fine.

MICHAEL. The Israelis have the military on high alert. Hamas is in the streets, calling for a new intifada.

HOWARD. Jerusalem, they're saying. That was the final thing for the Israelis. Everything else they could agree on except Jerusalem.

MICHAEL. I think there were actually a couple of things, but.

HOLLY. That fucker Arafat. Clinton gave them everything they wanted, they still couldn't say yes.

MICHAEL. It's a little more complicated than that.

HOLLY. *(To Ellen.)* I forgot. He loves the Arabs.

MICHAEL. What happened at Camp David, it was a lot, it was a much more complex situation than what you see on CNN.

HOWARD. I'm sure that's true.

MICHAEL. I mean, the Palestinian, so-called, "Palestinian state," that Clinton and Barak put forward—the Israelis would continue to have full control in terms of militarily, in terms of borders…

HOLLY. *(To Ellen.)* The things he says sometimes, if I didn't know him, honest to God, if I heard him on the street, I would think he was an anti-Semite. Honest to God.

MICHAEL. I'm a Jewish Studies professor.

HOLLY. When was the last time you went to synagogue?

MICHAEL. When was the last time you went?

HOLLY. We were at Washington Hebrew for Yom Kippur.

MICHAEL. You go twice a year, Holly. Which is two times more than I go. You're not exactly the Rebbe here.

HOLLY. I went for Sukkot last year, thank you very much.

MICHAEL. I'm an atheist just like you.

HOLLY. I am not an atheist, excuse me.

MICHAEL. Do you believe in God?

HOLLY. That has nothing to do with it.

HOWARD. Bombs is what scares me. Suicide bombs? Because these guys, they'll walk into a café, everything's fine, everyone's eating tuna sandwiches and drinking espresso, chit chat, and then it's, all of a sudden, you know, body parts and…it's just awful. Blood everywhere. Arms. They find people's arms. Or legs. Two hours later, a block away, they'll find a leg. That's what I'm, I just don't want that sort of thing to start happening again, because that is just…you hear the screaming and…bones and…

> *Beat.*

HOLLY. What the fuck are you talking about?

HOWARD. That's what they do.

HOLLY. Why would you say that? Their daughter is there, Howard. / Abby is there.

HOWARD. / They blow themselves up. It's scary as hell.

MICHAEL. I don't think anybody on either side wants dead American kids on the news.

ELLEN. Can we maybe not talk about dead American kids right now?

HOLLY. That would be nice, wouldn't it?

MICHAEL. By the way, where is Sharon? Speaking of suicide bombers.

HOLLY. *(Laughing.)* You are so bad. She had a book sale at school.

HOWARD. Hey. Congratulations on the book, Mike. That's fantastic.

HOLLY. How about a glass of wine? Am I the only one who wants a glass of wine?

ELLEN. I'm OK with coffee for right now.

HOWARD. *(To Michael.)* That's a huge accomplishment. To write a book?

MICHAEL. Thank you.

HOLLY. I always want a glass of wine. Is that bad?

HOWARD. This is your first book?

MICHAEL. Third book. The other ones have been a lot more specialized. So.

HOLLY. Unreadable.

MICHAEL. Well, I wouldn't say that, but.

HOLLY. I would.

MICHAEL. They weren't intended, they were written for academics. They were not for a general audience.

HOLLY. What's this one about?

MICHAEL. Do we really have to have this conversation?

HOLLY. What conversation? What did I do now?

MICHAEL. I just, I'm not good at the two-sentence, like, "This is a book about, you know…" I just, I hate that.

HOLLY. It doesn't have to be two sentences. Who said two sentences? What is he talking about?

MICHAEL. It's Jewish history. It's about Jewish history.

ELLEN. Well, that was two sentences.

HOLLY. *(To Ellen.)* Have you read it?

ELLEN. He won't let me.

MICHAEL. I want her to see it when it's finished.

ELLEN. He sent the manuscript to your dad six months ago.

MICHAEL. That was different.

HOLLY. You sent it to Dad? He must have been so touched.

MICHAEL. He never got back to me. So. I guess he wasn't that touched.

HOLLY. You're kidding.

HOWARD. Has he read it?

MICHAEL. I have no idea.

HOLLY. Have you asked him?

ELLEN. He won't ask him.

HOLLY. You haven't asked him? Ask him.

MICHAEL. I sent it to him. It's his prerogative, if he wants to talk about it—I'm not going to force him to talk about it.

ELLEN. I don't see why you can't just ask.

MICHAEL. Because I shouldn't have to ask.

HOLLY. I'll ask. Do you want me to ask?

MICHAEL. I really actually wish that you wouldn't.

HOLLY. It's crazy. Six months?

ELLEN. Michael actually has some other news, too.

HOLLY. Really?

Michael sighs, wishes she hadn't brought it up.

MICHAEL. I, um, I've been recommended for tenure. Starting in the fall.

HOLLY. I thought you already had that.

MICHAEL. No.

HOLLY. Well then, great.

Beat.

What?

MICHAEL. It's sort of a big…it's a big deal.

HOLLY. It's great. I just said that.

HOWARD. Really great.

MICHAEL. Most people, they don't, it's not an easy thing to accomplish.

HOWARD. I'll bet.

HOLLY. What are you teaching next year? Anything I'm interested in?

MICHAEL. Uh. I'm teaching a grad seminar on ethics in the Rabbinic literature. I'm doing the freshman survey course I do every fall about

Jews in Europe in the nineteenth century…

HOLLY. I'm already asleep.

MICHAEL. Thank you.

HOLLY. I liked the class you did on Jews in the movies. That's my kind of thing.

HOWARD. Mike, I've been reading, have you checked out the new Reagan biography yet?

MICHAEL. I haven't.

HOWARD. I think you would really, the guy is a sensational writer.

MICHAEL. *(Uninterested.)* Really.

HOWARD. Well, see, but I'm a big non-fiction guy, so that sort of thing is right up my alley anyway.

HOLLY. *(To Michael.)* Do you miss Mom?

MICHAEL. Do I what?

HOLLY. Do you miss Mom?

MICHAEL. Uh…

HOLLY. I miss her so much. Every day. It's like a piece of my heart has been ripped out. That's how I feel. Isn't that awful?

MICHAEL. I, yeah, I do miss her, Holly. It's kind of a random thing to bring up out of nowhere, but.

HOLLY. How is that random?

ELLEN. Maybe I will have a glass of wine.

    Ellen goes to the kitchen.

HOLLY. You sound like Jennifer. "Random." Everything I say is "random." "That's so random, Mom."

MICHAEL. It's just, it's a very personal question to just throw out there when we're sitting here talking about Ronald Reagan.

HOLLY. What did you think about Dad? Be honest.

MICHAEL. Wow, you just switch gears, don't you?

HOLLY. Do you see how thin he is? Didn't I tell you? He looks so old.

MICHAEL. He is old.

    Ellen enters from the kitchen, bottle in hand.

ELLEN. How's Riesling? That's all that's here.

HOLLY. Anything.

MICHAEL. I'll have a glass too.

HOWARD. None for me.

    Ellen begins to pour three glasses.

I can't drink it. It's too sweet.

HOLLY. Sharon spends all her time with him. Do you know this?

MICHAEL. Dad?

HOLLY. They go shopping together, they see movies. They're like BFFs. As Joey says. She's constantly at the house. The way she walks around now, you should see it, she picks things out.

MICHAEL. What does that mean?

HOLLY. She says, this is mine, I'll take this, I'll take that. I want the silver, I want the crystal. She's gone through Mom's jewelry already, you know that, right? You should be very concerned about this, Ellen. We're not getting a thing.

ELLEN. Oh, it's your mother. She didn't like me very much either.

MICHAEL. *(Half-hearted.)* She loved you.

HOLLY. *(To Ellen.)* She didn't love you. But that's not your fault.

MICHAEL. Mom loved Ellen.

HOLLY. She was very upset when you didn't convert.

ELLEN. I offered to convert. Michael said, no.

MICHAEL. Why would you convert to a religion for a spouse who doesn't believe in it?

HOLLY. She puts sticky notes on things. Sharon? On the bottom of furniture, the backs of paintings. With her name on them.

MICHAEL. Sticky notes?

HOLLY. The store, though, that's what she really wants. She's got her eye on that store.

MICHAEL. The store? Dad's store?

HOLLY. She's made friends with the family there, the Mexican family that rents it. She takes Dad there to see them every Sunday.

MICHAEL. Why would she even want it? I thought it was a ghetto dollar store now.

HOLLY. Do you have any idea how valuable the real estate there is these days? We're talking: mega.

HOWARD. It's up-and-coming, that whole area. 14th Street. Lots of new stuff coming in. Condos, retail.

HOLLY. Howard and I, we got in touch with an architect about it. You cannot breathe a word of this to Sharon. I'll kill you if you talk to Sharon about this. I mean it.

MICHAEL. You're talking to an architect about the store?

HOLLY. Did you hear what I said?

MICHAEL. I heard you, yes.

HOWARD. We've been discussing renovations…

HOLLY. The store hasn't been renovated in, like, a hundred years. All the systems need updating. All the plumbing, electric…

MICHAEL. Who's going to pay for that?

HOLLY. I'm going to pay for it. We're going to pay for it.

MICHAEL. Why would you do that?

HOLLY. Well, it's the perfect place for my business. Howard thinks so, too.

HOWARD. There's a lot of potential there.

MICHAEL. What is your business?

HOLLY. What do you mean, what is my business? Interior design.

MICHAEL. You do interior design?

HOLLY. Yes, I do interior design. You know that. I did the whole, I redid our entire house, top to bottom. And I did Sharon's apartment.

MICHAEL. That's not really a business. That's more like a hobby.

HOLLY. Well, because I don't have an office. The store would be my office. I could actually start something.

HOWARD. She's got a terrific eye.

MICHAEL. Have you talked to Dad about it?

HOLLY. Sharon has got him so in love with this Mexican family, he wants to keep them there forever, paying like two hundred dollars a month. Meanwhile, we could be making that store so beautiful,

Mikey.

MICHAEL. Where is Sharon's boyfriend in all of this?

HOLLY. Dumped her.

ELLEN. Oh no. Poor Sharon.

HOLLY. She left the temple she was going to. You know that. The temple she joined after Mom died?

MICHAEL. The Orthodox one?

HOLLY. It wasn't Orthodox. It was Conservadox.

MICHAEL. Right.

HOLLY. She got, she was very involved. And then all of a sudden, she broke up with the boyfriend, that was it with the temple. She took Dad there, too, all the time.

MICHAEL. I don't like her doing that.

HOLLY. Oh he got a lot out of it.

MICHAEL. He doesn't even read Hebrew.

HOLLY. She was going to get him into a class there.

ELLEN. Abby wants to learn Hebrew when she comes back.

HOLLY. Fabulous.

MICHAEL. Why is that fabulous? I don't understand that. Why is everyone, why are we excited about this?

HOLLY. It's wonderful. It's keeping the tradition alive.

MICHAEL. Which tradition, exactly?

HOLLY. (To Ellen.) He has to contradict everything.

MICHAEL. It's not her tradition. It's not, our grandparents, Mom's parents, do you think they spoke Hebrew? They didn't even go to temple. They were educated people. They were enlightened, cosmopolitan people. Now everyone is suddenly, I don't know what happened. What happened? Everybody's religious now?

HOLLY. So what?

MICHAEL. The head of my department—and this is a smart guy, this is not, this is a world-renowned scholar—he grew up like us: cheeseburgers, sweet and sour shrimp, Christmas trees—remember, we had that Christmas tree?

HOLLY. I love Christmas trees.

MICHAEL. Now, his whole family, they're *shomer shabbos*, they're walking to synagogue on Saturday mornings.

HOLLY. Why does that upset you?

MICHAEL. Because we spent the entire twentieth century trying to get away from that. And now you look around and everybody on the Upper West Side is reading books on Kabbalah and kosher sex, whatever the hell that is, and it's just, what happened to the last hundred years? Didn't we already have this conversation? Didn't we decide we were done with, you know, spirits in the sky?

ELLEN. I think you could be a little more tolerant of other people's beliefs.

HOWARD. I know what he's saying. I understand what you mean, Mike.

HOLLY. No, you don't.

ELLEN. The pendulum swings in one direction and then it swings back the other way. The parents are religious, so the kids rebel by giving it up. Then their kids rebel by going *back* to it.

MICHAEL. So history is just an endless repetition of the same? Back and forth?

ELLEN. The families I work with, I see it every day, the same patterns repeating themselves...

MICHAEL. Then how does anything new happen? How does anything change?

ELLEN. Maybe it doesn't.

HOLLY. He doesn't believe in tradition, Ellen. You're talking to the wrong person.

MICHAEL. I do believe in tradition. I just don't believe that religion, organized religion, is necessarily part of that tradition.

HOLLY. Of course you don't.

MICHAEL. A hundred years ago, Jews were part of every single radical, secular political movement in Europe. The Zionists? They hated religion. They hated the rabbis more than the communists did. The point was to change *this* world. To make a world where Jews wouldn't even exist—there would just be one single international human brotherhood. And then at a certain point, we just, we gave up. We gave up on politics and social justice, because…I don't know why. Because it was difficult. Because it didn't always work. So now we're just, we're running back into the arms of the most irrational, the most superstitious, reactionary forces, we're running as fast as we can back into the dark ages. Back behind our borders and our fences and our walls. Willingly. By choice. With eyes wide open. So, no, I'm sorry, I don't see that as keeping the tradition alive—Abby learning Hebrew. Not our tradition. Not my tradition.

    Beat.

HOWARD. We're sure there's just the Riesling?

Three.

    The guest room.
    Michael and Sharon sit beside the bed, a box filled with old photographs and children's drawings on construction paper between them.

SHARON. *(Handing him a drawing.)* Oh this one is my favorite. Read this one. I love this one.

    Michael reads.

MICHAEL. "Dear Mommy, I'm sorry I did a bad to you."

SHARON. I love that.

MICHAEL. "I wish you were not so mad at me now. Love, Mikey."

SHARON. I mean, is that not, how adorable were you? "Did a bad"?

MICHAEL. I don't find this adorable. I find this troubling.

SHARON. Oh I love it.

MICHAEL. I should show this to a therapist. This is, like, the smoking gun.

SHARON. A lot of these are like that. Apologies.

MICHAEL. I remember just constantly apologizing as a child.

SHARON. Mom used to say, do you remember? "I can forgive, but

I can't forget"—do you remember that?

MICHAEL. Of course.

SHARON. You can't say things like that to a five-year-old.

MICHAEL. You can, actually. You just shouldn't.

SHARON. I'm grateful, though. You know? That she was tough on us? These kids I teach, you should see the parents. Terrified of their own children. Tiptoeing around them.

MICHAEL. What do you think they're like in New York?

SHARON. There are pictures, too, see? Tons of old pictures…

> Sharon pulls a stack of photographs from the box, handing them to Michael.
> She points to one.

Dad behind the cash register.

MICHAEL. Probably the only time in his life.

SHARON. I know. I can't believe Mom let him stand there long enough to have his picture taken.

MICHAEL. Look at the fear in his eyes.

> They laugh.

SHARON. She could be sweet, though. Mom?

MICHAEL. Oh, when she was happy with you, there was nothing like that. It was like the clouds parting. Choruses of angels.

> They smile at the memory.

SHARON. I emailed you. Last week. I don't know if you got it.

MICHAEL. No, I did. I'm sorry. I've been swamped.

SHARON. I keep calling you. I don't hear back.

MICHAEL. Things have been crazy with work and moving into the new place…

SHARON. I just never know, are you getting the messages or am I, did I call the wrong number?

MICHAEL. I'm sorry.

SHARON. Well, I was just trying to see if you wanted to visit the store tomorrow, you and Ellen. I thought that might be fun if we all went. I'd love to introduce you to the Jimenez family…

MICHAEL. Oh. Yeah. Maybe. I don't know what time we need to head back to the city, is the only problem.

SHARON. We've become very close with them. Dad especially. They love Dad. It's adorable. They think he's, like, a legend.

MICHAEL. That's sweet.

SHARON. I think they saved his life. Honestly? He was not, I could barely get him to leave the house after Mom died. Finally one day, I decided, I'm taking him to the store. He hasn't been there in ten years. He just collects the rent checks in the mail. He should see it. He should meet his tenants. He'd never even met them.

MICHAEL. Right.

SHARON. He and Rod, they hit it off right away. Talking about the Orioles and the neighborhood…

MICHAEL. Rod?

SHARON. Rodrigo. He's the one that, it's his store. Well, he runs it with his son, Eduardo.

Michael nods.

You would love it. Being there. You walk in and it's just…you can feel it. All that history.

MICHAEL. I thought it was a bargain store now.

SHARON. Well, but I mean, so much of it is still there, though. The old moldings. The tin ceilings. And in the back, it's like it's frozen in time. There's an old framed picture of Kennedy hanging up…

MICHAEL. *(Stopping her before she goes on.)* I tend not to connect very much with places. Old houses, old buildings.

SHARON. Well, but some places, though, you can feel it. Like a spark of something…

MICHAEL. Yeah, see, I've never found that to be true.

SHARON. Well I won't beg you but…I think you would love it. I think you would really get a lot out of it.

MICHAEL. Maybe.

Beat.

SHARON. Did Holly tell you about Jonathan?

MICHAEL. Jonathan?

SHARON. Jonathan.

 Michael shakes his head, he doesn't know.

We dated for a year? *Over* / a year.

MICHAEL. / No, right. Jonathan. Yes. No, I did. I was sorry to hear about that.

SHARON. Well, I hope you know that it wasn't your fault. I don't know if Holly told you that it was, but it wasn't.

MICHAEL. Why would it be my fault?

SHARON. Um. For calling him a Nazi. At the funeral?

MICHAEL. I called him a Nazi?

SHARON. Yes, Michael. You said, you were talking to him, and he was telling you about his job, in marketing—and you went on this twenty-minute, on and on, about Hitler and the media, and complicity, how he needed to think about complicity...

MICHAEL. And that's why you broke up?

SHARON. No. I'm saying that's *not* why we broke up. If you thought it was.

MICHAEL. I would never have thought that.

SHARON. Well, he was very upset by that conversation. It rattled him. To be called a Nazi? It really, that really got to him. He started questioning everything. His career, our relationship, his faith...

MICHAEL. I don't even remember the conversation.

SHARON. He slept with our cantor. That's why we broke up.

MICHAEL. You're kidding.

SHARON. Please don't tell Holly that. I know you and Holly, you repeat everything I say—

MICHAEL. What?

SHARON. Come on, Michael. I know how you two, it's fine. It doesn't bother me. I get it, I'm just / asking you not to in this particular...

MICHAEL. / Then don't tell me things like that, Sharon. If you don't trust me, why would you tell me that?

SHARON. I do trust you, I just, I don't want you to tell Holly.

MICHAEL. I won't tell Holly.

SHARON. She lords things over you. She loves that.

MICHAEL. So what happened with…?

SHARON. Jonathan?

MICHAEL. Jonathan. What happened with Jonathan?

Sharon sighs.

SHARON. Well, Jonathan and the cantor, they're both…obsessed with Bruce Springsteen, and so that was, they were always, after services, they were always finding a table together at the oneg to talk about the "Boss," how much they loved the "Boss," what a great "Boss" the "Boss" was. And then, fast-forward to two months ago, and I walk in to my apartment and there they are on my bed.

MICHAEL. Jesus.

SHARON. Yeah. Oral sex. At the same time. Sixty-nine. On my bed.

MICHAEL. That's probably more than I needed to know.

SHARON. And this is the kicker, do you know what he said?

MICHAEL. I really don't.

SHARON. "It's not what it looks like." Do you like that? Sixty-nine on my brand new duvet cover, four hundred dollars, now I have to get it dry cleaned, which is going to cost me seventy-five, and it's not what it looks like. I mean, can you even…?

Beat.

MICHAEL. Was she a good cantor?

SHARON. She wasn't great, frankly. She was very nasal.

MICHAEL. I told you he was a Nazi.

Sharon smiles.

SHARON. Stop.

MICHAEL. I did.

SHARON. Stop it.

MICHAEL. I warned you.

SHARON. I should have listened.

MICHAEL. You can do so much better than that guy, Shar.

SHARON. I've gotten fat.

MICHAEL. What are you talking about?

SHARON. I have.

MICHAEL. You're, like, emaciated.

SHARON. Well, thank you, but…

MICHAEL. That's not a compliment.

SHARON. You look great.

MICHAEL. I stopped working out.

SHARON. I can't tell.

MICHAEL. I got one of those rollers from TV. Ab roller.

SHARON. Does it work?

MICHAEL. I don't know. I haven't opened it.

 Sharon takes in the room.

SHARON. I never come in this room anymore. Whenever I'm at the house. Too many memories, you know? Mom.

MICHAEL. It reminds me of being fourteen and smoking pot out the window.

SHARON. You know, the hospice people, they were going to set it all up in her room. They just assumed, but…she wanted to be here. In Mikey's room. No surprise.

 Beat.

MICHAEL. If you want help cleaning out some of this stuff…

SHARON. We already got rid of most of it. All the rental stuff. The hospital bed.

MICHAEL. You still have her clothes in the dresser…

SHARON. I'm not throwing out her clothes. I'm not ready to do that.

MICHAEL. What about the wheelchair? Do you really need the wheelchair? You need her prescriptions?

SHARON. I'm not ready.

 Beat.

I like knowing it's all here. It's like…it feels like everything is just sitting here, waiting for her to come back. Like she just went downstairs to make herself a cup of tea.

MICHAEL. I don't remember Mom ever drinking tea.

SHARON. Well, with the chemo. It's all she could keep down. Peppermint tea and Lorna Doones.

> *Beat.*

You were lucky. You missed a lot of that.

MICHAEL. I was working.

SHARON. I know.

MICHAEL. I'm not good in that sort of...I didn't want to see her like that.

SHARON. No one wanted to see her like that. We still did, though.

MICHAEL. OK.

SHARON. She understood. She really...I mean, you know Mom. Her son could do no wrong.

> *Beat.*

Dad looks good, doesn't he?

MICHAEL. Holly thinks he looks thin.

SHARON. She is so full of shit. He's put on ten pounds since last year. He was like a skeleton when Mom died. He practically killed himself trying to take care of her. Those last few weeks, he barely left the room. He wouldn't sleep, he wouldn't eat...

MICHAEL. It was probably the only time in their marriage when they got along.

SHARON. Don't say that.

MICHAEL. It's true.

SHARON. Now he goes to that McDonald's drive-through in Bethesda all the time. I can't get him to stop.

MICHAEL. He's still driving?

SHARON. *(Nods.)* His eyesight has gotten terrible. He sees double.

MICHAEL. Well, that's not ideal.

SHARON. I would really, I would love you to talk to him, Michael. Whenever I try to talk to him about things like this, he shuts down.

MICHAEL. If he's not listening to you, why would he listen to me, Sharon?

SHARON. He respects you.

MICHAEL. I'm not sure that's true actually.

SHARON. Oh come on.

MICHAEL. I sent him the manuscript of my book. Six months ago. He never responded.

Beat.

SHARON. I know.

MICHAEL. He told you?

Sharon nods.

What did he say?

SHARON. You know what? You should ask him. It's not my place.

MICHAEL. What did he say, Sharon?

Sharon sighs.

SHARON. He was hurt. He found it...hurtful.

MICHAEL. He found it hurtful.

SHARON. It's inflammatory, Michael, a lot of what you've written is very inflammatory.

MICHAEL. He told you it was inflammatory?

SHARON. He told me that, and then when I read it, / I agreed.

MICHAEL. / You read it?

SHARON. He gave it to me to see what I thought.

MICHAEL. Uh-huh.

SHARON. Look, I'm your biggest fan. You know that. But I was, honestly? If you want me to be honest with you? It's...I mean, it's offensive, Michael.

MICHAEL. You were offended.

SHARON. Yes.

MICHAEL. How were you offended?

SHARON. Um. Jews run the government? / Jews run the media?

MICHAEL. / Where do I say that? Where is that in the book?

SHARON. The Holocaust is about making money? Jews making money off of the Holocaust?

MICHAEL. OK. I'm sorry, Sharon, but that is an incredibly facile reading of an actually quite complicated argument.

SHARON. What did you think was going to happen? You thought that Dad was going to just, he was going to really respond to a book like that? You knew that it would upset him.

MICHAEL. It's a very personal book for me. I thought maybe he would appreciate that.

SHARON. Well, it felt like an attack. Like a personal attack.

MICHAEL. On Dad?

SHARON. On Dad. On our family.

MICHAEL. How is it an attack on our family?

SHARON. Obviously you hate where you come from, you hate the culture that you come from.

MICHAEL. That's not true.

SHARON. Well, I gave it to my rabbi and he / was…

MICHAEL. / You gave it to your rabbi?

SHARON. I have a very close relationship with my rabbi.

MICHAEL. This is the rabbi from the synagogue with the cantor? The sixty-nining cantor?

SHARON. He was as upset about what happened as I was, OK? He tried to fire her, and then the board…she did this whole song and dance for the board…

MICHAEL. And what did your rabbi think about my book? I'm sure he had a wonderfully sage response.

SHARON. Well, he said, in the Talmud, they talk about, if you slander your fellow Jew, that's one of the most, that's an unforgiveable crime, Michael. That's one of the worst crimes that there is.

MICHAEL. OK.

SHARON. I'm just telling you what he said.

MICHAEL. That was, just so you know, that was completely inappropriate of you to do that.

SHARON. To do what?

MICHAEL. That was an unpublished, that was a manuscript of a book, *my* book, which I sent to *Dad*, not to you, and certainly not to your asshole rabbi.

SHARON. OK. That is not fair, Michael. Abby told me about the petition against you. So obviously he's not the only one who felt that way.

Beat.

MICHAEL. When did you talk to Abby?

SHARON. Abby and I talk almost every day.

MICHAEL. Since when?

SHARON. She started calling me when she was in the hospital.

MICHAEL. Abby called you from the hospital?

SHARON. *(Nods.)* She needed advice, and I guess she felt like I was the easiest person for her to talk to, about the sort of things she was thinking about.

MICHAEL. And what was she thinking about?

SHARON. Life. Everything. Religion. God. Judaism.

MICHAEL. So you've been encouraging that?

SHARON. Why wouldn't I encourage it?

MICHAEL. Because her parents, you're not her parent, Sharon, and her parents don't approve of those kinds of values.

SHARON. Actually, Ellen has been very supportive. I'm not sure why you're so against it…

MICHAEL. Because I raised her as a secular, to be a secular person. A rational person.

SHARON. It's been very healing for her. She was almost…I mean, in November?

MICHAEL. What did she tell you about the petition?

SHARON. She told me that people read your book / and they started a petition to get you fired.

MICHAEL. / See, that's actually not true. Nobody has read my book. The book doesn't come out until October. The only people that have read the book are you and Dad.

SHARON. And Rick.

MICHAEL. Who's Rick?

SHARON. My rabbi.

39

MICHAEL. Rabbi Rick?

SHARON. So you're not worried that there's a petition against you?

MICHAEL. It's not even... Some disgruntled right-wing under-graduates read a two-page excerpt of the book, which they took completely out of context, and they came up with this idiotic idea for a petition. Well, you can't fire a tenured professor. I've been recom-mended for tenure. Do you even, did you know that? Did Abby tell you that?

SHARON. I thought you already had it.

MICHAEL. Well, I didn't.

SHARON. Well, mazel tov, then.

MICHAEL. Thank you. So much.

SHARON. How many people have signed it?

MICHAEL. Not very many.

SHARON. Fifty?

MICHAEL. I don't know. Maybe. Around there.

SHARON. More than fifty?

Michael stands.

MICHAEL. I should go check on Ellen.

SHARON. Please don't go. I don't want to fight with you.

MICHAEL. Neither do I.

SHARON. I need to tell you something.

MICHAEL. OK.

Beat.

SHARON. You're just going to stand there?

MICHAEL. I guess not...

Michael sighs and sits.

SHARON. You can't tell Holly.

MICHAEL. I won't tell Holly.

SHARON. I think I like someone.

MICHAEL. OK.

SHARON. Please don't tell this to Holly.

40

MICHAEL. I'm not going to tell Holly.

SHARON. I think it's… It feels like maybe it's…I don't know. I just feel so…I'm happy, you know?

MICHAEL. That's great, Sharon.

SHARON. Yeah. No. It is.

MICHAEL. Who is it?

SHARON. Well, so, actually…it's Rod. Rodrigo. That's sort of the, uh, funny thing about it.

MICHAEL. Rodrigo from the store? The Mexican bargain store?

SHARON. They're not Mexican, they're Guatemalan.

MICHAEL. Isn't he, how old is he?

SHARON. Fifty-one. It's twelve years. It's not that big a difference.

MICHAEL. So he's, what? He's divorced or…?

SHARON. They have a terrible marriage.

MICHAEL. Oh my God, Sharon.

SHARON. They hate each other.

MICHAEL. With children. They have children.

SHARON. Forget it. Forget I said anything.

MICHAEL. Sharon.

SHARON. No, if I knew you were going to just sit there and judge me, I wouldn't have told you.

MICHAEL. I'm not judging you. I'm telling you, this is a bad idea.

SHARON. Why did I even, I knew you'd be like this. / I knew it.

MICHAEL. / Like what? Like sensible? Like reasonable?

SHARON. Like you always are. Like you know everything and everybody else is a moron. Like I'm a moron.

MICHAEL. This is a family, Sharon, that you're getting involved with here.

SHARON. I don't care.

MICHAEL. You don't care?

SHARON. *(Steely.)* I don't care.

> *A knock on the door.*

Holly enters.

HOLLY. What are you fighting about?

SHARON. No one's fighting. We're talking.

HOLLY. Howard kicked me out of the kitchen. I've been exiled from the kitchen.

SHARON. Uh-oh.

HOLLY. I've been accused of micromanaging the table setting. Those are the charges against me. I'm a micromanager.

Holly sees the box of photographs and drawings.

What are these?

SHARON. Old drawings and pictures. Mom had them by her bed.

HOLLY. Is this the house? With the tree in front?

MICHAEL. It's the store.

SHARON. How do you know?

MICHAEL. Because I drew it.

HOLLY. It looks like the house to me.

MICHAEL. No. See the, uh, it has the man trying on clothes?

HOLLY. Is that what that is? I thought that was a baby.

SHARON. I thought it was a little puppy dog. With the tail here?

MICHAEL. What tail?

SHARON. The tail. See the tail?

MICHAEL. That's a suit jacket.

HOLLY. Wow. You were a terrible artist, weren't you?

Sharon and Holly laugh.

It's nice to be all of us together, isn't it? The kids. I don't remember the last time this happened, all of us here together. At the house.

SHARON. The funeral.

HOLLY. Has it really been that long?

SHARON. That was the last time Michael was home.

HOLLY. *(Pulling out a photograph.)* Oh my God. Here's Mom. Look how young she is.

Michael takes the photograph, looks at it.

MICHAEL. With a cigarette on her lip.

Holly examines a drawing.

HOLLY. Poor Mom. I miss Mom. Do you miss Mom, Sharon? Michael doesn't miss her.

MICHAEL. What? I never said that.

HOLLY. I thought you said you didn't miss her.

MICHAEL. When did I say that?

HOLLY. I don't know. I thought it was weird, too.

MICHAEL. But I didn't say it.

HOLLY. Oh. Well, good.

MICHAEL. Obviously, I miss her.

HOLLY. We all miss her.

MICHAEL. I know.

SHARON. Maybe she's here, too. Today. In spirit.

HOLLY. That's sweet, Sharon. To think that.

SHARON. Don't you ever feel that way? Like, you're walking up the stairs and suddenly you just feel this…sort of…presence? Like someone's right there next to you?

HOLLY. A little maybe. I think a little.

SHARON. I do.

HOLLY. That's nice. Do you, Michael? Do you ever feel that?

Michael looks at the photograph.

MICHAEL. No.

Four.

The living room.
After dinner.
Everyone brings glasses of wine with them, as Lou sits on the sofa with a small glass of scotch.
Howard nurses a beer.
Holly finishes clearing dishes from the dining room table.

Joey sits alone at the table, fixated on his Game Boy, with a can of Arizona iced tea.

ELLEN. She says the food is out of this world.

SHARON. It's like nowhere else.

ELLEN. She had the best falafel.

SHARON. Nowhere else.

Holly takes away the can of iced tea.

JOEY. I wasn't finished.

HOLLY. You're going to be up all night again.

ELLEN. She was in Tel Aviv, they went to this little hole-in-the-wall place. She said, Mom, you wouldn't have any idea it was even there, this place. No sign.

HOWARD. Those are always the best.

MICHAEL. Falafel is originally, it's actually an interesting history, in terms of the politics of falafel.

HOLLY. *(Laughs.)* The "politics of falafel"? That is not a real thing…

MICHAEL. It is, actually. The Israelis claim it's an Israeli food, the Palestinians say it's a Palestinian food…

HOWARD. Boy, they are just divided on everything over there, aren't they?

LOU. Ask Clinton.

HOWARD. Yeah. Ask Clinton. He'll tell you. They can't even agree to disagree.

LOU. The Arabs, they were never going to be happy with anything.

SHARON. Absolutely.

MICHAEL. Well, as long as Israel refuses to even discuss the concept of a right of return…

SHARON. Oh so you think, if it was up to them, they would give you that right?

MICHAEL. Why should I have that right?

HOLLY. Bite your tongue.

44

SHARON. Jews have one country. How many countries do they have? They can go anywhere. We have one.

HOWARD. I heard it was Jerusalem. That was the main, no consensus on Jerusalem.

MICHAEL. There is a consensus actually. There are eight different UN Security Council resolutions / on the subject.

HOLLY. / Oh, the UN—real Jew lovers.

SHARON. They want to cut up the city. Divide it up into parts. That's not a city anymore. That's just pieces.

MICHAEL. Much like the proposed Palestinian state.

ELLEN. Let's maybe talk about something else.

HOLLY. Wouldn't that be nice?

MICHAEL. I didn't bring it up.

      Pause.

HOWARD. I think McCain could have done something great / there.

HOLLY. / We're not talking about it anymore, Howard.

HOWARD. I was saying one thing.

HOLLY. It's over.

ELLEN. Dinner was delicious, Holly.

HOLLY. Oh stop.

HOWARD. You outdid yourself, honey.

ELLEN. I need the recipe for that green bean casserole.

HOLLY. Oh my God. It's so easy.

SHARON. It's Mom's recipe.

HOLLY. Mine is a little different.

SHARON. It tastes just like Mom's.

HOLLY. Hers was all from a can. I use fresh.

ELLEN. Well, it was delicious.

MICHAEL. It was great.

JOEY. I could probably do a tablecloth trick right now and pull the tablecloth out.

HOLLY. We're not doing that.

45

JOEY. I could probably do it though.

HOLLY. I don't care if you can do it, you're not doing it.

HOWARD. *(To Michael.)* He loves magic.

MICHAEL. Oh good.

HOLLY. *(To Joey.)* I am not asking you again. Put the Nintendo away and sit with your family.

> Joey sighs and puts down the Game Boy.
> He sulks into the living room.

HOWARD. Come join us, Joey.

SHARON. Holly, why don't you finish the dishes later? We're all relaxing now.

HOLLY. I need to let these soak.

SHARON. *(To Michael.)* She can't stop.

> Michael stands with his empty glass.

MICHAEL. Does anyone else need wine?

SHARON. I'll have a drop.

> Michael takes her glass, goes into the dining room for the bottle.
> At the table, he takes the cell phone out of his pocket, glances at it.

ELLEN. So. Do you feel seventy-five, Lou?

LOU. *(Shaking his head.)* Seventy-five. What a fucking nightmare.

HOLLY. Dad. Please, with the language.

SHARON. *(Seeing Michael studying the phone.)* Are you expecting a call?

MICHAEL. Abby has the number in case there's an emergency.

JOEY. Is that a cell phone? Can I see it?

MICHAEL. It's low on battery.

JOEY. Can I still see it?

HOLLY. He doesn't need to see it.

ELLEN. Why don't you put it away?

MICHAEL. I'm worried I'm not going to hear it.

ELLEN. Give it to me. I'll hear it.

Michael hands her the phone.

JOEY. That's what I want for my birthday.

HOLLY. You're not getting it. You're not a drug dealer.

ELLEN. Sharon was saying, maybe we could all go to the store tomorrow.

HOLLY. *(Glances to Michael.)* Really?

SHARON. Well, Dad and I, we're there on Sundays anyway…

MICHAEL. *(Making eyes at Ellen.)* Yeah, I don't know if that's, I mean, we can try, but…

ELLEN. I'd love to go.

MICHAEL. Well, but we have a train to catch, though.

HOWARD. The Acela, is it the Acela? You can exchange your ticket for a later one. No charge. I've done it a hundred times.

SHARON. Perfect.

MICHAEL. Great. Thanks, Howard.

ELLEN. Poor Abby. She's going to be jealous she missed out.

SHARON. *(To Howard.)* You guys should come, too.

HOLLY. *(A look to Michael.)* Maybe.

JOEY. I'm busy.

HOWARD. I don't think Joey's ever been.

JOEY. I'm busy, though.

HOWARD. What are you busy with?

JOEY. Extracurriculars.

HOLLY. *(To Joey.)* We grew up there, your uncle and I.

JOEY. Yeah, I know.

HOLLY. We'd go there after school. Do our homework in the back.

SHARON. Do you know about the store, Joey? Have you told him about the store?

HOLLY. Of course. He knows all about it.

SHARON. Do you know what it was called, Joey?

JOEY. No.

HOLLY. Yes you do. Yes he does.

LOU. Haberman's Corner.

JOEY. Oh right. I knew that. I already knew that.

SHARON. Your grandmother's family, they were the Habermans. And it was, your Grandma Mimi, her father, Papa Bill, your great-grandfather, he bought it all the way back in…when did he buy the store, Dad?

LOU. Who knows?

MICHAEL. 1880s.

LOU. Could be.

SHARON. And so when Grandpa, when he came back from the war, and he married Grandma—

JOEY. *(To Lou.)* Were you in the Marines?

LOU. Army.

JOEY. Marines are the best, though. They have swords.

HOLLY. Your grandfather liberated Dachau.

JOEY. Oh cool.

ELLEN. Incredible.

HOLLY. That's a big deal, Joey.

LOU. Well, there were a lot of us.

SHARON. And so when Grandpa married Grandma Mimi, after he came back, he started working in the store with Papa Bill. Menswear. Suits, ties…

HOLLY. They sold clothes to black people, Joey. Remember? I told you about this?

LOU. We sold to all kinds. We didn't care.

MICHAEL. Predominantly black people.

LOU. This was 1947. In Washington, the blacks, they couldn't go into any of the department stores.

ELLEN. That's incredible.

LOU. At Haberman's, we had good merchandise, we carried what they wanted, we had fair prices, and we didn't care what color you were. It didn't matter to us.

MICHAEL. A lot of the stores in black neighborhoods were owned

48

by Jews. Historically. Because they were cheaper to own and there was a captive customer base.

LOU. This was not a black neighborhood. It was a mixed neighborhood.

SHARON. And the Habermans hated you, didn't they, Dad?

LOU. The Habermans were German. They'd been in Washington for two generations already. My family, we were Russian, right off the boat. So we were...they looked down on us. They were snobbish. That's OK.

ELLEN. So after Papa Bill died, you took over the store?

Lou nods.

HOLLY. Well, with Mom. Mom worked the register, she did the bookkeeping...

JOEY. What happened?

LOU. What happened? Martin Luther King died, so the blacks had a riot, and they burned down the city. That's what happened.

MICHAEL. The blacks had a riot. All of the black people, apparently, on the planet had a riot.

LOU. Every street, they burned down, all the way up to our street.

HOWARD. Wow.

LOU. By the time they got to us, they were worn out, I guess. Stokely Carmichael had already gone to sleep maybe.

MICHAEL. By the time they got to you, the National Guard was there.

SHARON. It's like in the Exodus story. When God passed over the houses of the Israelites.

MICHAEL. Is it, though?

SHARON. I think it's very much like that.

HOLLY. *(To Michael.)* We were there that night. Do you remember?

Michael nods.

ELLEN. I didn't know that.

Michael nods.

HOLLY. We walked there after school, the two of us. And when they announced it on the radio, the assassination, Mom and Dad, I remember they looked at each other like...they knew. They just... knew. Dad took out all the money in the safe and he took out all the books from our bags, our school bags. And he put the books in the safe and he put the money in our bags. And he said, sorry about the books, we'll get them later. *(To Lou.)* Do you remember this?

Lou nods.

You decided—Mom was so mad—Dad decided, he was going to stay until things calmed down. So we locked up. Mom put down the grate. And I remember, we looked back inside, and Dad was just sitting there, listening to the radio. I'll never forget that. He stayed there all night.

Pause.

ELLEN. *(To Michael.)* You never told me about that.

SHARON. I don't remember where I was.

HOLLY. You were a baby. You were home with the nanny.

JOEY. *(To Lou.)* Why did you sell the store?

LOU. I didn't sell the store. We lease the store.

HOWARD. Your grandfather rents the store to people who pay rent for it, Joey. They pay him rent every month so they can use it. That's how rent works.

JOEY. Why don't you just run the store?

LOU. I'm too old to run a store. I don't have the energy.

HOWARD. It takes a tremendous amount of work to operate a business, Joey. Very time-consuming.

LOU. I got tired of all the bullshit. After the riots. The blacks were always mad about something after that.

MICHAEL. OK.   HOLLY. Dad.

HOWARD. The city changed. The whole country changed.

ELLEN. Probably for the better, in many cases.

MICHAEL. Most cases.

LOU. Oh it changed. A lot of drugs. A lot of guns. Homeless people.

HOWARD. Well, it's changing again. The neighborhood? All those new apartment buildings, new restaurants. The rents in that part of the District, they have shot up.

LOU. Yeah.

SHARON. We don't want to raise the rent. Dad loves the tenants we have now. We're going to have them for Rosh Hashanah this year. They've never been to a Jewish holiday.

MICHAEL. They're in for a treat.

SHARON. You should see Dad with Rodrigo. They have such a good time together.

LOU. He's got my sense of humor.

MICHAEL. Which is what?

LOU. Funny.

SHARON. Dad and I actually, last week we opened a college savings account for Eduardo's daughter, Silvia. She's seven. She's adorable. So smart.

HOLLY. You're paying for her college now?

LOU. *(Shrugs.)* It's a couple hundred bucks a year.

SHARON. She's brilliant, this girl.

ELLEN. How lovely.

HOWARD. I'm going to grab another beer. Anyone else for a beer?

HOLLY. I need water. With ice.

HOWARD. Coming right up.

Howard excuses himself to the kitchen.

LOU. And when I go, Joey—

HOLLY. God forbid, Dad.

SHARON. *(To Holly.)* Oh he loves to talk like that. He thinks it's cute.

LOU. No, someday, after I go, the store will be yours.

JOEY. Probably I'll make it a video game store.

HOLLY. No you're not, Joey.

JOEY. Do you know how much money you can make in a video game store?

MICHAEL. You're going to have to split it with Abby and your sister.

JOEY. That's fine.

HOLLY. *(Rolls her eyes.)* He's so generous.

SHARON. We'll see what the Jimenezes think about that. They have their own plans, I'm sure.

HOLLY. It's not their store.

SHARON. I didn't say it was.

LOU. *(To Joey.)* When my father, when he came to this country, he was your age. Didn't speak a word of English. He didn't go to high school, he didn't go to college. He came here with the clothes on his back.

ELLEN. That's amazing.

LOU. When he walked into Haberman's Corner, this was a man who spent his entire life living paycheck to paycheck. Everything he did, all the things he gave up, it was all for that. To live long enough that he could see that. That his son *owned* something. That there was something, brick and mortar, something you could touch, something to pass on to the next generation, something better than what came before.

SHARON. Wow, Dad.

HOLLY. Do you hear what he's saying, Joey?

JOEY. No, Mom, I'm deaf.

HOLLY. Nobody here thinks that's funny.

SHARON. The Jimenez family, they have the same story. They came here for a better life. For their children and their grandchildren.

MICHAEL. It's the immigrant's story.

LOU. I always thought that one of you kids would want the store, but you were too busy.

MICHAEL. We had careers.

LOU. Well, so.

     Pause.

HOLLY. Speaking of careers, Michael actually has some big career news, don't you, Michael?

MICHAEL. We don't have to do this.

HOLLY. Can I tell everyone?

MICHAEL. I think everyone already knows.

HOLLY. Michael got tenure, Dad.

LOU. Oh.

MICHAEL. Well…

HOLLY. Isn't that great?

LOU. Great.

SHARON. Good for Michael.

MICHAEL. Thank you.

ELLEN. We should toast.

SHARON. Absolutely.

HOLLY. He has a new book coming out, too.

MICHAEL. Let's not talk about the book.

HOLLY. Did you know Michael has a new book, Dad?

MICHAEL. I don't need you to do that.

SHARON. Let's talk about something else.

HOLLY. Well, but you were concerned, Michael—Michael was very concerned, Dad…

MICHAEL. What are / you…?

HOLLY. / Because he sent the book to you six months ago and he didn't hear anything back.

MICHAEL. What are you doing, Holly?

SHARON. *(Changing the subject.)* So Joey. Are you excited to start eighth grade?

JOEY. I'm starting eleventh grade.

> *Howard enters with a fresh beer and a glass of water for Holly.*

HOWARD. Are we talking about the book? Did I miss it?

MICHAEL. No, we're not.

HOWARD. Give us the, uh, the synopsis, Mike. Synopsize it for us.

HOLLY. Well, Dad read it. Maybe Dad can tell us about it.

SHARON. He doesn't want to talk about it.

HOWARD. I at least want to know the title. Can I hear the title?

MICHAEL. It's called, *Forgetting the Holocaust.*

HOWARD. Whoa.

HOLLY. Oh.

HOWARD. So it's about the Holocaust? Sort of a history?

53

MICHAEL. It's about Jews. American Jews.

HOWARD. And the Holocaust...

MICHAEL. The relationship between American Jews, Israel, and the Holocaust, how that relationship works.

HOWARD. Aha.

SHARON. *(Thinking it's over.)* Great.

HOWARD. And how does it work? The relationship?

MICHAEL. It works, uh, because Israel and the right-wing allies of Israel in this country, in the United States, they use the Holocaust, the memory of the Holocaust, to get American Jews, to support certain kinds of policy prerogatives in the Middle East.

SHARON. Is it fact or opinion? Because it sounds more like opinion maybe.

MICHAEL. I have sixty pages of footnotes.

HOWARD. That is impressive. Wow.

MICHAEL. I mean, why do you think both political parties in this country are in lockstep with whatever Israel wants? Why is that the one thing they can all agree on? Because of the goodness of our leaders? Because they love Jews so much? They didn't love us while the Holocaust was actually, you know, *happening.*

SHARON. Maybe it's because they understand that it's the right thing to do.

MICHAEL. Or maybe it's because they get campaign contributions from wealthy Jews and wealthy Jewish foundations, and that's what drives American foreign policy.

SHARON. He sounds like Pat Buchanan.

MICHAEL. Because Jews, who used to care about civil rights, social justice, economic justice, they're now, the number-one issue, the only issue, is Israel.

HOLLY. *(Stunned.)* This is what your book is about?

SHARON. *(To Holly.)* You know there's a petition against him. Do you know about the petition?

HOLLY. There's a petition?

MICHAEL. It's like a hundred people.

SHARON. You said fifty.

ELLEN. I think it was very brave of Michael to write about a subject like this. I think it took a lot of courage.

SHARON. Well, you're not Jewish, Ellen.

HOLLY. Sharon.

SHARON. So. Not to be rude, but, I'm not sure you really understand what these issues mean to people.

MICHAEL. Right. Because only Jews are allowed to have an opinion on Israel. / Everybody else has to just shut up and agree.

SHARON. / This isn't about opinions, Michael. This is about, Ellen has never had to worry about being put in a concentration camp because she's Swedish.

ELLEN. Norwegian, actually.

MICHAEL. And there it is. Thank you, Sharon, for demonstrating the entire thesis of my book. The best way to win an argument about Israel? Change the subject back to the Holocaust.

SHARON. If you don't understand the Holocaust, / how do you understand Israel?

MICHAEL. / The Holocaust has been used, the idea of the Holocaust, to distort American Jewish life, and discourse, and culture, since the 1960s.

SHARON. Here we go.

MICHAEL. Until today, now, it's now, I mean, go into any synagogue in America, the Holocaust is now the centerpiece of Jewish life. The lynchpin that binds us together is suddenly, it's not culture anymore or food or religion—it's certainly not religion, with the number of American Jews that actually practice their religion—it's the six million. And we've been manipulated, all of us, our entire lives, to feel constantly victimized, constantly afraid. You hear it all the time: "It could happen again, never forget, because it could happen again."

SHARON. Because it could happen again.

MICHAEL. It already has happened again. It happened in Bosnia, it happened in Rwanda. It just didn't happen to *us*. We learned all the wrong lessons from the Holocaust. We learned that the world hates Jews, that the world will always hate Jews, instead of what we should have actually learned—that nationalism is a sickness and it is lethal. And the book argues that the only way we can escape what has essentially become, at this point, a religion and a culture of frankly death and death worship, a culture that finds its meaning and its reason for being in the charnel houses of Europe, the only way we can get past that is if we forget it. Actively. We stop making movies about it and writing books about it, celebrating it, venerating it like it's this, like it's, it's—because otherwise, if we don't, I feel, I argue, at length, in the book—if we don't forget the Holocaust, now, if we don't begin to disentangle ourselves from our own obsessional neurosis, then we'll be, that's the end of us, this will be our last chapter. As a people. If we can even call ourselves that anymore, when the only thing that connects us to one another, that connects us to ourselves even, are ghosts.

> *Silence.*

I don't believe in ghosts.

Five.

> *In the living room, Michael sits in front of the television, his face creased with worry.*
> *Lou enters.*

LOU. Mind if I join you?

MICHAEL. No. Not at all.

> *Lou limps into the room.*

Do you need a hand?

LOU. No. No. I'm OK.

> *Lou sits.*
> *He sighs.*

The hardest thing is sitting down or standing up. You have to pick one or the other and just stick with it.

> *Lou takes the remote.*

Can I...?

MICHAEL. I'm not really watching.

Lou shuts off the TV.

Beat.

LOU. Sharon and I, we went to the cemetery last week. Did I tell you that?

Michael shakes his head.

We put a stone for you. For your mother. Told her you said hello. I meant to tell you that.

Beat.

MICHAEL. Thank you.

LOU. It's a nice spot. It's busy, it's always busy. That's what your mother liked about it. Right in the middle of the action. That's what she used to say. When we visited her parents. Right in the middle.

MICHAEL. I remember.

LOU. Well, you don't want to be somewhere quiet. Somewhere tucked away. Bushes and that sort of thing. You want footsteps. You like to hear footsteps.

Beat.

You got tenure. You never said anything.

Michael nods.

That's an accomplishment.

Beat.

I didn't know about this, uh…this petition either.

Beat.

A hundred people?

MICHAEL. Close to that.

LOU. How close?

Beat.

MICHAEL. The last I checked, it was, uh, it had just passed nine thousand signatures.

Beat.

I was recommended for tenure. The board hasn't…the board still has to approve the recommendation. They have to vote on it and…

Beat.

LOU. I did read your book.

MICHAEL. I heard.

Beat.

What did you think?

Pause.

LOU. At Dachau, I don't know if you came across this in your research or not, but when the Americans liberated the camps at Dachau—you have to remember, they didn't know what we know now. They didn't have a word for what they were about to see, to walk into. They thought it was a POW camp. Maybe forced labor, poor conditions, sure.

Every door they opened, every room, the floor to the ceiling, they found bodies stacked up, one on top of the other. You can imagine the smell. Coming from everything. From the gas chambers. From the bricks of the crematorium. The ovens. From the dirt under your feet even. On your boots. The ones we found, the ones who were still alive…it was the worst with them, the smell. Coming from off their skin, their breath. And they were so hungry, Michael. The GIs gave them food, rations. Some of them, they were so hungry, they ate it so quickly, no one could get them to slow down. And so their stomachs ruptured. After all those years and they ended up dead of a full stomach.

But some of them, they weren't hungry. They didn't want to eat. They didn't care about that, food. They went back and they found the guards, the Germans, and they rounded them up. They took shovels, they found shovels and bricks and sickles, and they hit them with the shovels, with the bricks, and the sickles. The Germans who killed their parents or maybe their brother or their children, right in front of them. The Germans with full stomachs, uniforms starched. They took the shovels, men who didn't weigh a hundred pounds, you could see the bones sticking out of their skin, they took the shovels and they smashed their faces in over and over again. On and on. And the Americans, the GIs, some of them even…they helped. They herded them together, the guards, they herded them up together, and they gave their guns to the prisoners and the prisoners shot them one by one. Like animals. Like Jews.

58

The Americans, they just watched. We just, we stood and we watched. And we were glad. My God. We were glad. I'm still glad.

Pause.

For you, history is an abstraction. But for us, the ones who survived this century, this long, long century…there are no abstractions anymore.

Long silence.
Suddenly, the lights go off in the dining room and Howard, Holly, Ellen, Sharon, and Joey enter.
Holly carries a homemade birthday cake with ten candles on it into the dining room.

HOWARD, HOLLY, SHARON, and ELLEN. *(Singing.)* Happy Birthday to you.

HOLLY. Come on, Dad.

Lou and Michael go to join them at the table in the dining room.

HOWARD, HOLLY, SHARON, and ELLEN. *(Singing.)* Happy Birthday to you.

HOLLY. Sing it, Joey.

HOWARD, HOLLY, SHARON, ELLEN, and JOEY. *(Singing.)* Happy Birthday…

HOLLY & SHARON.	HOWARD & ELLEN.	JOEY.
Dear Dad	*Dear Lou*	*Dear Grandpa*

Ellen suddenly hears the phone ring in the living room.
She goes to get it.
Michael follows her.

ELLEN. Hello?

ALL. *(Singing.)* Happy Birthday to you.

MICHAEL. Who is it?

SHARON. *(To Michael.)* Does she need to get that right now?

JOEY. Can I blow out the candles?

HOLLY. It's not your cake.

HOWARD. Happy Birthday, Lou.

HOLLY. Make a wish, Dad.

LOU. I'm thinking, I'm thinking.

ELLEN. Honey?

MICHAEL. Is it Abby?

JOEY. Can I please blow out the candles, Howard?

HOWARD. Let your grandfather do it.

SHARON. Is Ellen on the phone?

JOEY. I have a wish, though, too.

HOLLY. No, you don't.

> *Sharon notices Ellen's distress.*

MICHAEL. It's / Abby?

SHARON. / What's going on?

ELLEN. I can't hear you, honey.

LOU. What is it, Sharon?

> *Joey blows out the candles.*

HOLLY. *Excuse* me.

JOEY. What?

HOLLY. What did I tell you?

MICHAEL. Where is she, Ellen?

HOLLY. Can you please get involved here, Howard? / For once.

HOWARD. / That wasn't nice, Joey.

SHARON. What's happening, Michael?

ELLEN. I can't hear you.

JOEY. I had a really good wish.

HOLLY. I don't care *what* wish you had.

MICHAEL. *(Silencing the room.)* Can everybody just…?

ELLEN. Slow down. I can't understand you, Abby.

> *A long beat.*
> *Ellen looks at Michael, her face ashen.*

MICHAEL. What happened?

> *Ellen slowly holds out the phone to him.*
> *Black.*

End of Act One

ACT TWO:
February 18, 2001

One.

A frozen winter morning.
The streets of Tenleytown are icy and wet, with huge banks of dirty gray snow pushed up against the curb.
The house is a mess: stacks of unopened mail piled up on the dining room table, prescription bottles everywhere.
Lou sits alone in the living room in a hospital chair, reclined, the television on in the background.
Sharon enters in a heavy winter coat, mail in one hand, a bag from the pharmacy in the other.

SHARON. I'm home. Finally. Oh my God. Terrible accident on Wisconsin.

Sharon comes from the dining room to the living room.

Dad? Are you awake? Oh. Hi. You are awake. Hi.

She turns off the television.

That is the worst intersection. At Albermarle? And people go through there like…they're driving sixty miles an hour. It's absurd.

Lou opens his mouth to respond.
Words do not come out.

Oh. Here. This doesn't look very comfortable…

She adjusts a pillow behind him.

How's that?

Sharon sits on the sofa, sorting through the mail.

I just spoke to Rod again. He says, they're all pulling for you, down at the store, the whole family. Eduardo wanted to come and bring you flowers. I said, Ed, what is Dad going to do with flowers? He doesn't need flowers. What he needs is, he needs somebody who can actually, he needs people here helping him, that's what he *actually* needs. Ed said, but aren't you helping him? I said, yes. He said, well, what about everybody else? I said, everybody else? Who's that? Oh, you mean, my siblings? Oh, they're busy, I said. They've got very busy, very important schedules, apparently, so. I'm just still, I know I sound like a broken record, but I'm still just a little unclear on what Holly has better to do right now.

Holly appears in the dining room, unseen by Sharon.

It's just, because, I have to go back to work eventually. I've already used up half of my vacation days. I can't just, I have a job. And Holly, meanwhile, she's sitting at home watching *Who Wants to Be a Millionaire?*

HOLLY. Hi / Sharon.

SHARON. *(Jumps.)* / Oh my God.

HOLLY. Did I scare you?

SHARON. Oh my God.

HOLLY. I'm sorry.

SHARON. Oh my God.

Sharon gestures to the pharmacy bag in the kitchen.

I was, um, I got refills on Dad's meds.

HOLLY. Did you save the receipt?

SHARON. I put it on his Mastercard.

HOLLY. You just left Dad?

SHARON. I was gone for fifteen minutes.

HOLLY. Really? Because I've been here for half an hour.

SHARON. He was sleeping when I left. And he has the Life Alert if there's an emergency.

HOLLY. I made up the guest room for Michael and Ellen.

SHARON. Oh. Thank you.

HOLLY. And I vacuumed.

SHARON. I've been meaning to vacuum all week.

HOLLY. Well now you don't have to.

SHARON. Now I don't. Good point.

Sharon laughs.

You scared me half to death.

HOLLY. I know.

SHARON. I thought I was going to have a heart attack.

> *Holly kneels by Lou.*

HOLLY. Are you thirsty, Dad?

SHARON. I've been giving him water all morning.

HOLLY. His lips are chapped.

SHARON. I gave him a glass of water literally an hour ago.

HOLLY. He needs to stay hydrated.

SHARON. *(Chagrined.)* Yes, I'm aware. Hence the water.

HOLLY. His lips shouldn't get chapped like this.

SHARON. They weren't chapped when I left.

HOLLY. Well, they're chapped now. So.

> *Holly holds out a juice box from the table.*

Here, Dad. Juice. Left hand. You have to practice.

> *She holds the straw from the box to his lips.*
> *He takes some.*
> *He spills a little bit.*

Oops. That's all right. That's OK.

> *She wipes his face.*

You OK? Do you want some more?

> *Lou shakes his head very slowly, pushing away her hand.*

OK, Dad.

> *Holly pats his hand.*

OK.

> *She tries to contain her emotion, as Lou stares off.*

SHARON. Guess who called this morning?

> *Beat.*

Guess who called, / Holly?

HOLLY. / I don't know, Sharon.

SHARON. Rodrigo. He's been calling every day.

HOLLY. That's nice.

SHARON. I know. Don't you think?

HOLLY. Mmm.

SHARON. He got Silvia on the phone yesterday. I put it on speaker for Dad. She was so sweet.

HOLLY. Mmm.

SHARON. It really makes his day. Hearing from them. Hearing from anyone.

HOLLY. I'm sure.

SHARON. How does he look? What do you think?

HOLLY. *(Lying.)* Good. He looks good.

SHARON. Better, don't you think? Better than last week?

HOLLY. Mmhmm.

SHARON. Good. I think so, too.

> *Sharon exits.*
> *Holly sits there, looking at her father.*

HOLLY. Much better.

> *She kisses him on the forehead.*

Two.

> *The guest room.*
> *Suitcases on the bed.*
> *The medical equipment is all still there.*
> *They speak in hushed voices, in media res.*

HOLLY. It's been a nightmare.

MICHAEL. How was I supposed to know that? Nobody told me that.

HOLLY. It's been an unending / fucking nightmare and it hasn't even been…

MICHAEL. / You told me, he couldn't talk, Holly. That's all anyone told me—he can't talk.

HOLLY. Well, he can't.

MICHAEL. It's more than he can't talk. He can't…he's not even, he just sits there.

HOLLY. Isn't it fun?

MICHAEL. Does he have any idea what's happening / or is he just…?

HOLLY. / Sometimes, yes. Sometimes, no. He's in and out. He gets confused, he forgets where he is…

MICHAEL. So cognitively, it's…

HOLLY. He can't dress himself, Michael. He can't feed himself. He can't go up the stairs. We have him sleeping on the pullout sofa in the office. He can't use the bathroom by himself.

MICHAEL. Jesus.

HOLLY. Yeah. It's all very good news.

MICHAEL. So what are we going to do?

HOLLY. What do you mean, what are we going to do?

MICHAEL. I mean, in terms of, does he need professional care? / Does he need…what does he need?

HOLLY. / Professional care? He's getting professional care. He's in physical therapy, he's in occupational therapy…

MICHAEL. Here, I'm saying. Somebody living here. Somebody full-time.

HOLLY. Maybe.

MICHAEL. What about Sharon?

HOLLY. What about her?

MICHAEL. Isn't she sort of, she's already living here, right? It seems like?

HOLLY. Are you saying we should hire Sharon to be Dad's nurse?

MICHAEL. No, I'm saying, maybe that's, if that's something she wants to keep doing for the time being…

HOLLY. Would you want to keep doing that?

MICHAEL. I'm not Sharon. I don't enjoy my own misery in quite the same way she does.

HOLLY. Oh, she's already complaining, she's already—I'm not doing anything, Howard's not doing anything…

MICHAEL. Well, I mean, OK, because otherwise, somebody who comes here, a live-in person, that's going to be, that's very expensive.

HOLLY. Yes. Thank you, Michael. We all know it's expensive.

MICHAEL. I'm just saying, I don't think that Medicare covers that kind of thing.

HOLLY. It didn't cover it for Mom.

MICHAEL. Right. So. Exactly.

HOLLY. You weren't there for most of that, I guess.

MICHAEL. Is that, are you guilt-tripping me now? About *Mom*? Really?

HOLLY. Do you *feel* guilty?

MICHAEL. I don't live here, Holly. It's a trek for me to get here. You live fifteen minutes away.

HOLLY. Thirty to forty-five, in traffic, actually.

MICHAEL. Well, you're a much better person than I am. What can I say?

HOLLY. Oh give me a fucking break, Michael.

MICHAEL. What do you want from me, Holly?

HOLLY. No, you show up here a week after the stroke—

MICHAEL. You told me you didn't need me. You and Sharon both, you told me not to come.

HOLLY. Well, because we knew how busy you were.

MICHAEL. Yes. I'm in litigation right now,/ I was in depositions all week.

HOLLY. / "Professional care"? What do you think we've been doing? Giving him aspirin and hot water bottles?

MICHAEL. If you had told me to be here, I would have been here the second I heard.

HOLLY. Woulda coulda shoulda.

MICHAEL. Fuck you.

HOLLY. Fuck you.

MICHAEL. No, fuck / you, Holly.

HOLLY. / No no. Fuck you, Michael. You fucking self-righteous fucking asshole.

A long, long silence.

How was the train?

Beat.

Did you take the train? How was the / train?

MICHAEL. / We took the bus.

HOLLY. Greyhound?

MICHAEL. Do you really care?

HOLLY. No. I don't.

Beat.

How are you?

MICHAEL. How am I.

HOLLY. I feel like I haven't spoken to you in months.

MICHAEL. We spoke yesterday.

HOLLY. For ten minutes.

Michael sighs.

MICHAEL. I'm terrific, Holly. Couldn't be better.

HOLLY. Are you being facetious?

MICHAEL. Yes. I am.

HOLLY. How's the job search going?

MICHAEL. *(Laughs.)* The job search. That's funny. I can't get a job anywhere in North America at this point. I have a publicist, though. I got a publicist. He gets me speaking engagements at left-wing colleges. And bookstores. Tiny bookstores.

HOLLY. That's fancy.

MICHAEL. It's not. Really.

HOLLY. It's better than nothing.

MICHAEL. It essentially is nothing. So. Minus five percent. For the publicist.

HOLLY. And the lawsuit, it's still…

MICHAEL. It's ongoing.

HOLLY. Have you thought about settling?

MICHAEL. Sure. They just need to reinstate me in my position. With lost wages. Plus, damages for defamation. And I want an apology, a public apology from the board, from the president. Then, sure, I'll settle for that. That's fine.

HOLLY. What do they say?

MICHAEL. What do they say. They say that my work lacks "scholarly rigor." That's their term of art: "scholarly rigor." Whatever that means, "scholarly rigor." Which, this is after the faculty committee voted unanimously to recommend me for tenure. Glowing reviews from students, fellow academics, but no. The board has decided that they know better. Only the second time, by the way, in the hundred-and-fifty-year history of the university that the board of trustees has refused to approve a tenure recommendation. What was the first time, you may be asking yourself? Oh. Well. The guy was accused of—and this is not a joke—accused of fucking a horse. So, in the annals of university history, it is now me and the horse fucker.

HOLLY. They didn't like the book?

MICHAEL. No. They did not like the book. They, uh, they disliked the book, I would say.

HOLLY. Well, is it selling at least?

MICHAEL. How is it supposed to sell if the publisher won't market it? I mean, it's like, you would think it never even happened.

Beat.

HOLLY. Sharon said Abby decided not to go back to school...

MICHAEL. When we took her in January, she couldn't wait to start classes, see her friends. Then we got a call from the emergency room three weeks later.

Holly shakes her head.

Before Israel, we didn't...we thought she had an eating disorder. Even when she was in the hospital last year. It was bad, but it was still...we'd seen bad. We didn't think it was some kind of actual... hearing voices, talking to herself, hurting herself, cutting herself...

HOLLY. Well, the cutting, sometimes they do that for attention.

MICHAEL. These were not, what happened in Jerusalem was—I don't know how much you actually want to hear this, Holly.

HOLLY. I want to hear it.

Beat.

MICHAEL. Uh, well, the depth of the cuts, the lacerations that she made, these were very, they were not…superficial.

HOLLY. Oh.

Pause.

MICHAEL. They told us it was Jerusalem Syndrome. Abby had a case of Jerusalem Syndrome.

HOLLY. *(Nods.)* Howard looked it up on the Internet.

MICHAEL. The hospital there, they said they see a hundred, hundred-fifty people a year with it.

HOLLY. That's a lot.

MICHAEL. Well, and it's especially…if people already have pre-existing, if they have certain trauma or emotional issues or, which obviously Abby…it can trigger, just being there in the city, people who aren't even religious, suddenly they're, they start seeing visions, scaring tourists.

Beat.

But if it was Jerusalem Syndrome, she's home, so why is she still… why isn't she OK?

Pause.

HOLLY. How's Ellen managing?

MICHAEL. Ellen? She's in complete denial. She spent the whole fall going with Abby to temple every Saturday. She thinks this is all…she thinks Abby is having a spiritual crisis. She wants her to talk to a rabbi. She wants her to *be* a rabbi. She doesn't understand that when Abby says she's having visions, when Abby says God is speaking to her, what she really means is, she's having a mental breakdown. It's not something to be encouraged. She's not Joan of Arc. Although, look at Joan of Arc. Imagine if she had been alive in the age of Wellbutrin and cognitive behavioral therapy.

Beat.

HOLLY. She thinks that…God is speaking to her?

MICHAEL. On occasion.

Holly nods, troubled by this.

HOLLY. Do you want some drugs maybe? It sounds like you maybe could use some drugs.

MICHAEL. What do you have?

Holly gets her purse.

HOLLY. Everything. I'm like a pharmacy. I have Ativan, Xanax, Valium, Klonopin.

MICHAEL. I'll have half a Xanax.

Holly gets the bottle out.

Where do you get all these?

HOLLY. They're prescriptions. I have anxiety issues. I'm being treated by many doctors. They don't know about each other. Here.

Holly hands him a pill.

Take the whole thing. You'll thank me later.

Michael swallows.
Holly takes two.

MICHAEL. This is just like old times. Me and my big sister getting high, listening to Jim Croce.

HOLLY. No Jim Croce this time.

MICHAEL. Too bad.

Beat.

What about you? How are things with you? Aside from the anxiety issues.

HOLLY. Things are all right. Well, until Dad.

MICHAEL. Yeah? Joey's...

HOLLY. Joey's OK.

MICHAEL. How's Howard?

HOLLY. Working like a maniac. He's been doing all of these big mergers, traveling all the time.

MICHAEL. Huh.

HOLLY. He got a computer for his birthday. Now he's obsessed with it. The Web. Whenever he's home, he's down in the basement on AOL. He goes on these family genealogy things, chat rooms.

MICHAEL. That sounds fun.

HOLLY. I think he's probably doing porno things. Is my hunch. Genealogies at four in the morning doesn't seem normal to me.

MICHAEL. Well but it is Howard, so.

HOLLY. I have something to show you. Look at this.

Holly hands him a business card from her purse.

I had them printed the other week.

MICHAEL. "Holly Fischer, Spaces and Places."

HOLLY. Everyone says, "interior decorator," "interior design." I thought, let's do something different. Let's do something fun. "Spaces and Places." Isn't that fun? It's fun, right?

MICHAEL. It's, yeah, it's very fun.

HOLLY. It's so fun. But, it's going to be very upscale. Very concierge. And this architect, we've been really getting into the plans. Especially since, when Dad got sick, I thought—um, hello? Wake-up call. We can't keep waiting on this. I know how much he loves that Spanish family, but you're talking about, we need someone living here with him, taking care of him? Well, guess what? He needs someone in that store who's going to pay real money.

MICHAEL. So you're going to pay rent to Dad?

HOLLY. Why not? I'll pay the actual, we'll pay the real price every month, not the discounted special. And Howard and I, we'll pay for the renovations, we'll pay for the upgrades.

MICHAEL. What does Sharon say?

HOLLY. Oh, Sharon is practically, she would cut my head off before she let me take the store away from these people. You should see how she is with that little Spanish girl. I think she finally realizes she's never going to have her own children. That's over and done with. So she might as well, this could be her little adopted daughter. It's sick.

MICHAEL. So you haven't brought it up with her?

HOLLY. Well I figured…I didn't want to say anything until I knew that you were on my side about it.

MICHAEL. Do I really have to pick a side?

HOLLY. I'm sorry, are you new to this family? Have you been in

71

this house before?

> *Michael goes to hand her back the card.*
> *She waves it away.*

That's yours. So, tell me more about your career. You're officially, that's it, you're fired, end of story?

MICHAEL. The university doesn't have an open position for me. That's the, uh, the party line. No open position.

HOLLY. Mmm.

MICHAEL. Because the Anti-Defamation League has nothing better to do apparently than turn me into their cause of the month, the self-hating Jewish Studies professor Hitler apologist who wants to wipe Israel off the map.

HOLLY. Wow.

MICHAEL. I mean, the bottom line is, they can't fire someone for saying something politically that they find noxious, so that's, this is how they do it. This is the playbook. They find some technical loophole. They use words like "scholarly rigor" so they don't have to say the truth, which is that academic freedom in this country does not extend past the Green Line, past 1967, let alone '48.

> *Beat.*

It's a dark time.

HOLLY. It sounds like it.

MICHAEL. For all of us. I mean, another Bush in the White House. A *second* intifada. Ariel *Sharon*, the butcher of Sabra and Shatila. History repeating itself, everything terrible coming back around but worse. And where are we in all of this? American Jews? We're just rah-rah-rahing alongside everybody else, the Bushes and the Cheneys and the Donald Rumsfelds of the world. Alan Greenspan— that's what's left. That's our inheritance. A hundred years ago, we had Albert Einstein. We had Emma Goldman. Hannah Arendt. Walter Benjamin. Now, what do we have? William Kristol? Alan Dershowitz? That's what remains of the great Jewish radical intellectual tradition? O.J. Simpson's defense attorney? Really? What happened to the red diaper babies? The Jews who sat at the lunch-counters and marched in Selma. Who burned draft cards and stormed the Pentagon. We were in the streets. We were shutting down traffic and disobeying police orders and refusing to be silent in the face of empire and death. But we traded in all of that for a seat at the table, didn't we? For Joe Lieberman on the presidential ticket. And look at us now. Now the whole world eats bagels. They watch *Seinfeld* in Topeka. We even have our own country, with our own atom bombs and everything, Star of David gunships. We're white people now. We're respectable. We're nothing. Nothing at all.

    Silence.

HOLLY. But…so, I can count on you though, with the store?

MICHAEL. Sure.

    Beat.

I'm starting to feel the Xanax, I think. My tongue is very heavy all of a sudden.

HOLLY. Take a nap.

MICHAEL. Maybe.

HOLLY. I'm happy you're here, Mikey.

MICHAEL. Don't call me Mikey. I hate that.

    Holly puts her hand on his knee.

HOLLY. I'm happy you're here. Michael.

    Beat.

MICHAEL. Me, too.

Three.

    The dining room.
    Joey sits reading the Guinness Book of World Records *at the table.*
    Ellen sits, unsure what to say.
    Lou remains in the living room, watching television quietly.

ELLEN. How's school?

JOEY. It sucks.

ELLEN. That's too bad.

JOEY. I'm used to it.

> *Beat.*

ELLEN. We saw your sister's play a few weeks ago. *The Seagull.*

JOEY. Mom said Jennifer had the smallest part in the show.

ELLEN. Well, she didn't say very much, but she was onstage a lot. Especially between scenes, moving things on and off...

JOEY. Is Abby coming today?

ELLEN. She isn't. But she sends her love.

JOEY. Is she living in a mental hospital?

ELLEN. Is she...?

JOEY. Howard said she has to live in a mental hospital.

ELLEN. She's in, it's called an outpatient program. She was never, she's not in a mental hospital.

JOEY. Howard said Abby went crazy in Israel.

ELLEN. Abby had, she was going through a very, a tough time. But she's doing a lot better. She's feeling really good now.

JOEY. Why isn't she here?

ELLEN. She had a lot of...she has a busy schedule.

JOEY. At the mental hospital?

ELLEN. Again, there's no mental hospital. There's an outpatient program.

> *Sharon enters from the kitchen, surprised to see Ellen.*

SHARON. Ellen. I didn't know you were here.

ELLEN. We just got in.

SHARON. *(To Joey.)* And you're here, too.

JOEY. Hi.

> *Sharon glances back at Lou.*

SHARON. *(To Ellen.)* How long has he been asleep?

ELLEN. Ten minutes?

SHARON. Do you think he's warm enough? I just turned the heat up.

ELLEN. No, I think he's, I think it's good.

74

SHARON. How's Abby?

ELLEN. She's, you know…she's doing OK.

SHARON. I spoke to her this morning.

ELLEN. Oh.

SHARON. She said she wanted to come today but Michael wouldn't let her. That's not nice.

ELLEN. Well, Michael felt it was better for her not to make the trip. All the added stress.

Sharon nods, skeptical.

SHARON. We should talk later. Privately.

ELLEN. *(Chagrined.)* OK.

SHARON. Abby's feeling very…she's upset with her dad. She thinks he's being very unsupportive.

ELLEN. She and I have already, we've had a lot of conversations about that. And it's, we've resolved the issue.

Sharon nods again, skeptical.

SHARON. Let's talk later.

ELLEN. *(Rankled.)* Great.

SHARON. I want to be as helpful as I can, you know?

ELLEN. Thank you.

SHARON. I love my Abby. I was there when she was born. Remember that?

ELLEN. *(With a laugh.)* I do. I was also there.

SHARON. *(Laughs.)* That's true.

Holly enters, frowns as soon as she sees Joey.

HOLLY. Why are you here?

JOEY. Howard dropped me off.

HOLLY. What is he doing?

JOEY. He said he had to run errands.

HOLLY. What errands?

JOEY. I don't know. Stop screaming.

Holly kisses Ellen.

HOLLY. Hi sweetheart. You look thin.

ELLEN. Oh. No.

Holly glances back at Lou.

HOLLY. Is he warm enough?

SHARON. I just turned up the thermostat.

HOLLY. God. I'm freezing. Are you cold, Ellen?

ELLEN. I'm OK.

SHARON. I don't want him to get overheated.

HOLLY. It's like an igloo in this house.

SHARON. Where's Michael?

HOLLY. I left him upstairs. He's taking a nap.

SHARON. I thought we were all going to talk as soon as he got here.

HOLLY. Well, he's tired. I gave him a Xanax.

SHARON. OK.

HOLLY. You know, I'm here, too, Sharon. I can talk. Why don't we talk?

SHARON. Yeah, let's talk.

ELLEN. Do you want me to…?

SHARON. I don't think we need you right now, Ellen. Is that OK?

ELLEN. Oh no. Of course.

HOLLY. Thank you, sweetheart. You're so sweet. *(To Sharon.)* Isn't she sweet?

SHARON. The sweetest.

HOLLY. So sweet of you to be here.

ELLEN. Should I get Michael?

SHARON. Not if he's napping. I bet he's tired from the long bus ride. That's very tiring. Sitting on a bus. Reading a book.

ELLEN. I'll see if he's up…

Ellen exits.

SHARON. She left Abby at home, alone with a nurse. They hired some nurse.

HOLLY. I thought Abby was in a mental hospital.

JOEY. It's an outpatient program.

SHARON. She begged them to come today. Begged. To see Dad?

HOLLY. That's sweet.

SHARON. Michael refused. Of course Ellen just rolls over.

HOLLY. Well, I think it sounds like things are very delicate with Abby right now.

SHARON. Is that what Michael told you?

HOLLY. I don't want to have this conversation in front of Joey.

JOEY. I'm not listening.

HOLLY. Go to the other room.

JOEY. You go to the other room.

HOLLY. Excuse me?

> *Joey sighs loudly and stands.*

Pull up your pants.

JOEY. I already did.

HOLLY. You look like a thug.

JOEY. I am a thug.

HOLLY. *(To Sharon.)* He doesn't even know what that means.

JOEY. Yes I do. I'm not retarded.

HOLLY. What did I tell you about saying that word?

JOEY. I know I know. Jesus.

HOLLY. Then don't do it.

> *Joey enters the living room, reluctantly sits beside his grand-father, eyeing him warily as he does.*

SHARON. That's smart. Not letting him say retarded.

HOLLY. Why is that smart?

SHARON. Well because it's...it lets him know that it's not a bad thing.

> *Beat.*

HOLLY. Joey is not retarded.

SHARON. I know that.

HOLLY. So why is it smart?

SHARON. You know what, Holly? If you're just going to pounce at everything I say...

HOLLY. We're supposed to be talking about Dad. Let's talk about Dad.

SHARON. I'm exhausted.

HOLLY. Well, you've been doing too much, Sharon. You're running yourself ragged.

SHARON. I can't just take off work forever. I have twenty-three kids that need me.

HOLLY. Of course.

SHARON. I just…I can't keep doing everything myself.

HOLLY. I've been here every day, Sharon.

SHARON. That's not true, but OK that's fine.

HOLLY. You're right. Thursday, I had a doctor's appointment.

SHARON. For the entire day.

HOLLY. *(Swallowing her annoyance.)* What is going to make you happy?

SHARON. We need somebody here with him. Twenty-four hours a day.

HOLLY. I think we all agree on that, Sharon.

SHARON. The sooner, the better.

HOLLY. Well, Howard looked at Dad's insurance. The long-term care? First of all, it takes three months for the coverage to even kick in.

SHARON. We can't wait for three months.

HOLLY. And then once it does kick in, Howard says it's crap.

SHARON. So where does that leave us?

HOLLY. *(As casually as possible.)* Well, I mean, obviously there's the store…

SHARON. The store?

HOLLY. Well, just in terms of, when you look at the money that's coming in…the rent that's being paid right now is very low, Sharon.

SHARON. That's what Dad wants.

HOLLY. Is that what Dad wants or what you want?

SHARON. It's what we both want.

HOLLY. Well, so if you're saying that you won't even *consider* the income that Dad is getting from the store…

78

SHARON. I won't.

HOLLY. Which is his primary, his *only* source of income…

SHARON. We're not raising the rent.

HOLLY. Well, then I don't really know the other option, Sharon. / I hate to tell you.

SHARON. / The other option is Howard, obviously. He makes more money than all of us combined.

HOLLY. We can help out.

SHARON. You can "help out"?

HOLLY. I'm not asking Howard to put in all of the money when we can't even have a conversation about the store. That's not fair.

SHARON. Fair is, we each give what we can afford. I can afford to spend time, helping Dad, and you and Howard can afford to pay for his care.

HOLLY. We would be paying for care so you *wouldn't* have to spend time helping Dad.

SHARON. I would still help Dad.

HOLLY. Then why would we pay for care?

SHARON. You know what? Forget it. This isn't worth it.

HOLLY. OK. Are we having a hissy now? / Is that what's happening?

SHARON. / No. Let's just let Sharon do everything. It's going to be just like Mom, all over again.

HOLLY. Excuse me?

SHARON. Because Sharon, what does she have better to do? She's just a kindergarten teacher with no life. She can stay with Mom and change her catheter and change her clothes…

HOLLY. *(Gathering her keys.)* No. I'm leaving. If you're going to be like this?

SHARON. *(To Holly.)* Where are you going?

HOLLY. I'll pick up dinner.

SHARON. I already got groceries.

HOLLY. I'll get more.

SHARON. That's a waste.

HOLLY. I know.

>*Holly exits.*

SHARON. Holly. Seriously?

HOLLY. *(From off.)* Seriously.

>*The front door slams shut.*
>*Sharon fumes.*
>*Beat.*

JOEY. Where did Mom go?

>*Beat.*

Aunt Sharon? Where did Mom / go?

SHARON. *(Snapping.)* / She left, OK? She's gone.

>*Beat.*

JOEY. OK.

>*Michael comes downstairs, looks into the living room.*

MICHAEL. What happened?

JOEY. Mom left.

MICHAEL. Where did she go?

JOEY. I don't know.

>*Beat.*

MICHAEL. How's it going?

JOEY. Fine.

MICHAEL. How's school?

JOEY. It sucks.

MICHAEL. *(Not listening.)* Great.

>*Michael looks at Lou.*

JOEY. He's asleep.

MICHAEL. I see that.

>*Michael goes into the dining room.*

Where did Holly go?

SHARON. I hear you're taking drugs.

MICHAEL. What?

SHARON. Holly gave you drugs, right? You're high?

80

MICHAEL. I took one Xanax. I am not high.

SHARON. We're not here to have fun with drugs, Michael.

MICHAEL. "Fun with drugs"?

SHARON. We need to figure this out.

MICHAEL. And I'm here to figure it out. What is your problem?

SHARON. My problem? I don't have a problem. I'm not the one who can't spend two minutes in this house without getting stoned.

MICHAEL. You know what? If you're going to be combative and rude at everything I say...

SHARON. No, I'm not, I'm sorry. I'm in a shitty mood. I'm sorry. I have the worst headache.

MICHAEL. Have you eaten anything?

SHARON. I am so nauseous right now.

MICHAEL. Are you sick?

SHARON. Holly put me in a shitty mood.

MICHAEL. You don't have to take it out on me.

SHARON. I know. You're right. I'm sorry. You're right.

>   *Sharon takes a breath, tries to start over.*

Thank you for coming. Thank you for being here. I know it wasn't easy for you.

MICHAEL. I wanted to be here sooner.

SHARON. Well still. You did your best.

MICHAEL. You did tell me you didn't need me.

SHARON. It's been a hard couple of months, I know. With Abby, and then this whole lawsuit business...

MICHAEL. Yeah.

>   *Beat.*

SHARON. I guess, maybe I was right, though. About the book?

>   *Beat.*

MICHAEL. What?

SHARON. Well, I told you people would be upset.

MICHAEL. I don't care if people were upset.

SHARON. Well, then, good.

MICHAEL. They should be upset. It's upsetting.

SHARON. It is upsetting. To tell people to forget the Holocaust.

MICHAEL. I didn't actually, that was not meant to be taken literally. Obviously. It was a provocation. An intellectual provocation.

SHARON. So you don't want people to forget the Holocaust?

MICHAEL. *(Struggling to explain.)* No, I do want people to forget the...I want people to remember in a different way...

SHARON. Why didn't you say that, then?

MICHAEL. That is what I said.

SHARON. No, you said, "forget."

MICHAEL. As a provocation.

SHARON. Well, I didn't get that.

MICHAEL. OK.

SHARON. It seems like, I think most people didn't get that.

MICHAEL. It does seem like that, doesn't it?

　　　Beat.

SHARON. What a shitty year it's been. All this shit. Abby, Dad...

MICHAEL. Well, then the Supreme Court. The coronation of George W. Bush. I thought that was going to kill me. On top of everything else. I started watching CNN until two, three in the morning, just yelling at the screen. Because if I can't yell at the board of trustees, I can at least yell at fucking Bernard Shaw.

　　　Beat.
　　　Sharon just nods.

Oh my God. You voted for him, didn't you?

SHARON. What? Who?

MICHAEL. You voted for Bush, didn't you?

SHARON. It's none of your business what happens inside the ballot box. That is private.

MICHAEL. Only Republicans say that.

SHARON. I'm an independent.

MICHAEL. I cannot believe that my own sister voted for George Bush.

SHARON. Just because you disagree with my opinions doesn't mean that you're right and I'm wrong.

MICHAEL. Well except in this case I think actually it does mean that.

SHARON. You didn't vote for Gore either.

MICHAEL. Well, I didn't think he was going to lose.

SHARON. I know this may not matter to you, but Bush happens to be much better for Israel.

MICHAEL. Better in what sense of the word?

SHARON. Uh. In the sense that he's not going to force them to give up Jerusalem like / Clinton was trying to do.

MICHAEL. / Clinton was—The Israelis would have kept all of West Jerusalem, two-thirds of East Jerusalem…

SHARON. You know, a lot of Democrats, a lot of liberals, people like you, have become frankly very anti-Semitic. Especially about Israel. And a lot of Jews are realizing that the Republicans? They actually *like* Jews. They *want* them in their party.

MICHAEL. Until they don't.

SHARON. Well, anyway, like I was saying, it's very kind of you to take time out of your busy schedule to be here a week after we needed you.

MICHAEL. You told me you didn't need me, Sharon.

SHARON. I'm so appreciative that you could be here with us today to help poison the atmosphere. You've already turned Holly into a nightmare.

The front door opens.

HOWARD. *(From off.)* Hello? Anyone home?

SHARON. Oh fabulous. Another big help.

MICHAEL. I'm here to be helpful, Sharon. That's why I'm here.

Howard comes into the dining room.

HOWARD. Hey Mike. How are you, buddy?

Handshake.

MICHAEL. Hi Howard.

HOWARD. Where's Holly?

SHARON. She stormed out of the house.

HOWARD. Ay ay ay. Is everything…?

SHARON. *(Sarcastic.)* Everything's great.

HOWARD. Hi Sharon. How are you, sweetheart?

SHARON. I feel like I'm going to vomit, Howard. How are you?

HOWARD. Pretty good. Can't complain. Weather could be / better.

SHARON. / So happy to hear that. I'm going to go sort Dad's pills for the week.

MICHAEL. We're not going to talk?

SHARON. How can we talk when Holly isn't here?

MICHAEL. Well, can I help you?

SHARON. No. Thank you.

>   *She goes.*

MICHAEL. Don't say I didn't offer.

SHARON. *(From off.)* I definitely will not say that.

HOWARD. *(Sotto voce.)* Is she…?

MICHAEL. Insane?

HOWARD. *(Laughing.)* Your words, not mine.

MICHAEL. Is there anything to drink in this house?

>   *Michael peers in the liquor cabinet.*

HOWARD. There might be some Kahlúa left over from Holly's birthday.

MICHAEL. I only see vodka.

HOWARD. That's it then probably. Sorry to say.

>   *Michael pulls out a big plastic jug of vodka, the kind college
>   students have.*
>   *He brings it to the table.*

MICHAEL. The first time I ever got drunk was vodka. Holly and I stole a bottle from my parents. We must have been, I was only twelve, but she must have been fifteen, I guess, sixteen. We split it one night when they went out for dinner. I threw up three times. Holly held her own.

HOWARD. Sounds like Holly.

MICHAEL. Sharon was nine. She caught us, ratted to Mom and Dad. Naturally.

> *He drinks, grimaces.*
> *He holds it out to Howard.*

I don't think it warrants actual glasses.

HOWARD. I'm all right, I think.

MICHAEL. You sure? It tastes terrible…

HOWARD. My parents, it's funny, they never drank. Holidays occasionally. I figured it was a Jewish thing.

MICHAEL. With our family, it was split down the middle. The Russians, they'd barely finish a glass of Manischewitz at Passover. But the Germans, they were all drunks.

HOWARD. That's fascinating.

> *Michael takes a big pull from the bottle.*

You're going to regret that later.

MICHAEL. I'm sure I will.

> *Michael takes another pull.*

HOWARD. Why don't you slow down, Mike? You're going to get drunk like that.

MICHAEL. That's the idea.

HOWARD. It's pretty early, don't you think?

MICHEL. I have to get drunk enough to beg you for money. So.

> *Howard laughs.*
> *Michael doesn't.*

HOWARD. Yeah?

> *Pause.*

You need…you need money, Mike?

MICHAEL. I'm about a hundred grand in the hole right now, approximately. Not to mention, two months late on the mortgage. So, yes. I do. I do need money.

> *Beat.*

I thought maybe you could float me a loan. I'll pay you back. I'm obviously—it's just, right now, it's, with the apartment, and the legal fees and Abby's, the treatment program, Abby's school which we're still paying for…

HOWARD. Have you thought about declaring bankruptcy?

MICHAEL. Yeah, I've thought about it.

HOWARD. And?

MICHAEL. And I thought I could get a loan from you so I wouldn't have to do that. That was my thought.

> *Beat.*

Look, this would just be a temporary—as soon as I win the case, I'm going to have, we are seeking major, major damages.

HOWARD. Well, but if you lose the case, Mike…

MICHAEL. No. No way. This is a fundamental First Amendment issue. They either, either we win in court, or they settle, and the settlement is…I mean, it's got to be high six figures for us to even entertain it. It's just, at the moment…my lawyers are delaying any more work until they get paid.

> *Beat.*

HOWARD. Boy. Boy oh boy. I mean, the thing is, God, it's just, cash is pretty tight for me right now, Mike.

MICHAEL. Uh-huh.

HOWARD. We're not doing so great ourselves at the moment.

MICHAEL. Yeah? It was a slow year for you?

HOWARD. It was actually.

MICHAEL. That's not what Holly thinks.

HOWARD. Holly doesn't know.

MICHAEL. Bush is giving you a tax cut, though, that'll be nice. Maybe bump you back up a little.

HOWARD. Hey, I voted for Gore.

MICHAEL. Well, good for you, Howard.

HOWARD. *(Trying to change the subject.)* I just couldn't wait for that damn election to be over. And then Florida. I couldn't believe everything that went down. With the chads and was it a hanging chad or was it a regular chad or… Could you believe that?

Michael just looks at him.

Can I, uh...?

> *Howard reaches for the vodka.*
> *He takes a big gulp from the bottle.*
> *He chokes.*

Oh God, that's really...

MICHAEL. You OK?

> *Howard takes another big gulp, chokes.*

Hey. You don't...

HOWARD. I made some, uh, I made some bad decisions, Mike. I made some pretty, uh...the past couple months?

MICHAEL. What kind of decisions?

HOWARD. Holly doesn't even...this has to be between you and me, Mike. Man to man. You have to promise me that.

MICHAEL. What kind of decisions, Howard?

HOWARD. *(Desperate.)* You have to promise me, Mike. Please.

MICHAEL. Jesus.

HOWARD. Promise.

MICHAEL. Yes. I will. I promise.

HOWARD. Because I just can't...

MICHAEL. I promise, Howard. Calm down.

HOWARD. I'm trying.

> *Beat.*

We got a, uh, we got a computer.

MICHAEL. I heard. Holly said you do genealogies.

HOWARD. Yeah. I mean, no. I don't.

> *Beat.*

I got involved with some...I don't know, just chat rooms, these chat rooms. Nothing actually, just some stupid sex talk bullshit, nothing big. Stupid.

MICHAEL. I think that's pretty common.

HOWARD. Yeah, no, I think, yeah. But then it started, I don't know,

I just, I got into it, Mike. I got really just…the whole experience. Nobody knows who you are, what your history is. You can be fat or thin or black or white or you can be a guy who's a girl or a girl who's a guy or… Am I freaking you out?

MICHAEL. Not yet.

HOWARD. I gave someone my credit card. I don't know why I even…we'd talked for hours online, I mean hours and hours. We met a couple times. She was, she had a hard life. She was from one of those…Estonia or Lithuania or… She wasn't a…a call girl or… she'd gotten involved in some things she wanted to get out of, but she was, they lock you into these things and you can't get out. So I said—I was *so stupid*. I was just so freaking stupid, Mike. I told her, I gave her my card number, I said do what you have to do, then get it back to me. And she did, she charged, you know, a couple thousand bucks on the card, and she said, yep, all done, thank you so much. And then she sort of disappeared. But then a week later, the phone rings and it's Mastercard and it was…I mean, tens of thousands of dollars, Mike. And I can't dispute the charges, because I *gave* her the card. So I canceled it. Problem solved. But then I got another call from Visa. And then another call from Discover. She used my information, she used my name and my information and she took out, she had twelve credit lines, all maxed out. Cash advances. We're talking, hundreds, OK? Hundreds of thousands just gone. Like that. Vanished. And it's not like, we didn't have a whole lot of savings to begin with. Everything I make, it goes right out the door. And what am I supposed to do now? If I tell them what happened, then they have to open an investigation, and if they open an investigation, Holly finds out, and if Holly finds out, I am fucked.

> *Beat.*

It was barely even sexual between us, is the thing. At least after the first couple times. I just, I liked her. I thought she was nice.

> *Beat.*

What do you think?

MICHAEL. What do you think?

HOWARD. About the situation…

MICHAEL. Uh. What do you think I think, Howard?

HOWARD. I don't know.

MICHAEL. This is my sister.

HOWARD. It's my wife.

MICHAEL. How am I supposed to react to this?

HOWARD. Like a friend maybe?

MICHAEL. I'm not your friend, Howard. I'm your brother-in-law.

Beat.

HOWARD. Well then never mind.

MICHAEL. "Never mind"? I can't just "never mind." How am I supposed to "never mind"?

HOWARD. If you had told me about something like this, I would have never-minded.

MICHAEL. Well except I didn't have sex with a prostitute from the Internet and give her my credit card, Howard. That was you. You did that.

Silence.

HOWARD. I did. You're right. I did.

Beat.

MICHAEL. What are you going to do?

HOWARD. I don't know.

MICHAEL. You don't know?

HOWARD. I don't know.

MICHAEL. That's not good.

Beat.

HOWARD. I had one idea. Maybe.

MICHAEL. What is it?

HOWARD. This can't come from me. Otherwise, Holly will just…

MICHAEL. What's your idea, Howard?

Beat.

HOWARD. The store.

MICHAEL. Are you talking about Holly's interior decorating business? Spaces and Spaces?

HOWARD. No.

MICHAEL. Because I don't think that's going to be some kind of cash / cow.

HOWARD. / I'm not talking about Holly's business, Mike.

MICHAEL. Then, what are you talking about, Howard?

> *Joey enters.*

JOEY. Hello.

> *He sits at the table and opens his book.*
> *Michael and Howard sit there in silence, waiting for him to take the hint.*
> *He does not.*

Four.

> *The dining room.*
> *Michael, Holly, Sharon, Howard, and Ellen sit at the table, in the middle of the discussion.*
> *Lou remains seated in the living room, alone, with the television on quietly.*

MICHAEL. I think we need to have some sense of overall cost before we start even talking about who's doing what.

SHARON. This is not about money.

HOLLY. It's a lot about money.

SHARON. I disagree.

MICHAEL. It has *something* to do with money.

SHARON. I think actually it has more to do with care.

MICHAEL. Right now, we need to know what each of us, what we're going to be expected to contribute here. In terms of, fine, care. Let's call it care.

SHARON. Well with Mom, for instance, what ended up happening was I did everything. From the beginning.

HOLLY. That is just not true, / Sharon.

SHARON. / I moved into the house the day she was diagnosed, and I left a month after the funeral. Two years of my life.

HOLLY. I was here as often as I could be.

SHARON. Which was not a lot. To just be, if we're being honest about it.

HOLLY. I had two children to raise.

MICHAEL. It doesn't matter who was here more.

HOLLY. Well, you weren't here at all. So.

MICHAEL. I really don't want to dredge this up.

SHARON. I bet you don't.

MICHAEL. Can we get back to Dad? Since that's what we're talking about. Please.

ELLEN. If I could just... In my experience with families that are... when there are health issues that affect everyone...a good question to start with is really, what *kind* of care do you think he's going to need?

SHARON. He's going to need someone here. Someone at the house.

ELLEN. OK. Great. That's very helpful. To guide the conversation.

MICHAEL. How much does that cost?

SHARON. A thousand dollars a week?

ELLEN. Wow.

MICHAEL. A week?

SHARON. At least.

MICHAEL. Ellen and I don't have that kind of money.

SHARON. Do you think I do?

ELLEN. I'm sure we can help...

HOLLY. Howard looked through Dad's savings.

HOWARD. There's not a huge amount of savings...

SHARON. He spent everything for Mom. Insurance wouldn't cover any of it. The prescriptions, the nurses.

HOLLY. Howard and I can obviously, we can take care of a lot of the costs. We have the most and so, that's fine with us.

SHARON. Good.

HOWARD. Well. Uh. There's not necessarily, with Joey, with his needs, we don't have unlimited resources.

SHARON. No one is saying unlimited, we're saying you're rich, you're a lawyer.

HOWARD. Joey is very expensive.

HOLLY. That is not a nice thing to say.

HOWARD. I didn't mean it like…come on. I'm saying, with his school…

HOLLY. He's our son.

HOWARD. A lot of our money is tied up. There's Joey's tuition, Jennifer's tuition, Jennifer's apartment, Jennifer's allowance…

HOLLY. Which we have already cut back on.

HOWARD. If it's not already with the kids, then it's tied up in investments. There's not a tremendous amount of cash just lying around for the taking.

> Holly glares at him, not sure what he's trying to accomplish with this.

MICHAEL. I wonder if maybe the best solution, there might actually be a best-case scenario here that we haven't even really thought about?

SHARON. Which is what?

MICHAEL. Uh. Well. The store.

HOLLY. Yes.

SHARON. What about it?

MICHAEL. Properties in that area have really…14th Street?

HOLLY. Everything there is hot right now.

SHARON. I'm not raising the rent on the Jimenez family.

MICHAEL. I'm not talking about raising the rent.

SHARON. If other property owners are doing that, pricing people out, that's despicable. To me? That's horrible.

ELLEN. I agree.

MICHAEL. I'm not saying raise the rent.

HOLLY. Michael is saying that it's time to consider new tenants. Tenants who can afford to pay the market price for rent.

MICHAEL. That's not exactly / what I'm saying…

HOLLY. / The Jimenez family is…they've been wonderful. But the store is a business, Sharon. We have to think about it like a business.

SHARON. Yes, I'm aware that it's a business, Holly, thank you.

HOLLY. I've been looking for office space for the past two years. Howard can tell you. I've looked everywhere, and the store…it's perfect. It's the perfect location…

SHARON. Office space for what?

HOLLY. My business.

SHARON. What business?

HOLLY. Well, it's called Spaces and Places…

SHARON. *(To Michael.)* What is she talking about?

MICHAEL. Let's maybe / take a second.

HOLLY. / It's a boutique interior design firm.

SHARON. I'm lost.

HOLLY. With the rent we pay Dad, Howard and I will end up paying for his care. That's the point, OK?

SHARON. We're going to kick out the Jimenez family so that she can have an office for a business that doesn't exist?

HOLLY. It does exist, Sharon. Do you want to see my business cards? *(To Michael and Howard.)* Can you please support me here, someone?

SHARON. *(To Michael.)* This is your idea, too?

HOLLY. *(Before he can respond.)* Yes, it is.

SHARON. You want to put the Jimenez family on the street after all they've done for Dad?

MICHAEL. Can I say / something?

HOLLY. / "All they've done for Dad." What have they done for Dad?

SHARON. Everything.

HOLLY. Like what?

MICHAEL. OK, before we get / too far ahead of ourselves…

SHARON. / Like lift his spirits.

HOLLY. By calling him on the phone once a week?

SHARON. By caring, Holly. By actually / caring.

93

HOWARD. / I think Mike is trying to say something.

MICHAEL. I'm saying, sell the store. We sell the store.

A long, stunned silence.

HOLLY. *What?*

MICHAEL. Now, before you both have your knee-jerk / reactions…

SHARON. / Absolutely not.

MICHAEL. Can you listen?

HOLLY. You want to *sell* the store?

SHARON. We're not doing that.

MICHAEL. It's not even "the store" anymore. It hasn't been "the store" in thirty years. It's a Mexican / bodega.

SHARON. / Guatemalan. And it is not a bodega.

HOLLY. *(To Howard.)* Are you going to participate in this conversation, Howard, or are you just, are you suddenly a deaf mute?

HOWARD. I'm listening to Mike. I want to hear what Mike has to say.

MICHAEL. This would guarantee that we have enough money for Dad, and then whatever is left over, we can, you know, we can divide the rest between us.

SHARON. So this is an investment thing for you?/ This is a moneymaking thing?

MICHAEL. / It's our inheritance. We're going to inherit it anyway. What's the difference?

HOLLY. The difference is, he's still alive, Michael.

MICHAEL. Well, and this way he could see us / enjoy the money, instead of just waiting until he isn't here anymore.

SHARON. / You want to sell the store to some huge real estate company, they're going to knock it down and turn it into some kind of what, condos for yuppies?

HOLLY. It's horrible.

SHARON. It's a neighborhood there.

HOLLY. It's a neighborhood. That's exactly right.

MICHAEL. It's not going to be a neighborhood for much longer. / This is the way things are going.

94

SHARON. / Oh so you're comfortable, Mr. Ralph Nader, you're comfortable completely transforming the face of this neighborhood?

MICHAEL. It's already happening. Whether we want it to or not.

SHARON. You're comfortable kicking Hispanic people out of their own neighborhood?

MICHAEL. It used to be a Jewish neighborhood. Then it was a black neighborhood. Now it's Hispanic. Soon it'll be something else.

SHARON. Wow.

ELLEN. I'm not comfortable with any of this.

SHARON. Thank you.

ELLEN. This is your family's heritage, this is Abby's heritage in that store…

MICHAEL. It's a building, Ellen. It's four walls and a ceiling.

SHARON. Our grandparents built those walls. They built the ceiling. They built the floors. / They built something there. For us.

MICHAEL. / I don't actually think, I'm sorry to burst your bubble, but I think the building was already there.

ELLEN. Abby would be heartbroken to lose that history.

HOLLY. How do you think Joey would feel? Or Jennifer?

HOWARD. They don't care.

HOLLY. That is absolutely / not true.

MICHAEL. / We could sell it for three to four million dollars, OK? That's the figure we're talking about. Just so we all, so we're all on the same page, OK? Three to four. Million.

> *Pause.*

HOWARD. You're kidding.

MICHAEL. Conservatively.

HOLLY. So what?

MICHAEL. *(Incredulous.)* So what?

HOLLY. I don't care if it's twenty million dollars.

HOWARD. It's a lot of money, Holly. Three million dollars?

HOLLY. We already have a lot of money, Howard.

ELLEN. Nobody needs that kind of money.

MICHAEL. Uh. We do. We're broke, Ellen.

ELLEN. We are not broke.

SHARON. No, we understand, Michael. Money comes first. Spoken like a true socialist.

HOLLY. Howard and I can give you money, Michael. If you need money?

MICHAEL. *(To Howard.)* Oh really?

ELLEN. We don't need money. Michael is exaggerating.

SHARON. Oh he's being very dramatic. / He's putting on a little show for us.

MICHAEL. / How am I exaggerating? What am I exaggerating?

ELLEN. We have my salary. You're completely discounting my salary.

MICHAEL. Your salary? Are you kidding?

ELLEN. Am I *kidding*?

HOLLY. I'm sorry but there is already a compromise here that everybody is ignoring. Which is: Spaces and Places.

SHARON. Oh my God.

HOLLY. We're offering, Howard and I are offering to take care of Dad. All of his expenses.

MICHAEL. Is that true, Howard?

SHARON. But you need something in return. You need your little... your project.

HOLLY. It's not a project. It's a business.

MICHAEL. This is what / you want to do, Howard?

HOLLY. Howard and I are going to renovate the store. We are going to update all of the systems. For free.

HOWARD. We should discuss the details first.

SHARON. Who's going to pay for that? He's not going to pay for that.

HOLLY. Of course he is.

HOWARD. Let's just, can we discuss for one second...?

SHARON. See?

HOLLY. Do you believe in this or not, Howard?

96

HOWARD. I believe in it, I just think that what Mike is saying, it makes a lot of sense to me.

HOLLY. Oh it does?

HOWARD. Three million dollars?

HOLLY. So nobody is on my side.

HOWARD. Of course I'm on your / side, Holly…

HOLLY. / Nobody is supporting me.

HOWARD. I'm just trying to think about it practically.

HOLLY. No, you know what? I give up.

HOWARD. Holly.

HOLLY. I give up. *(To Sharon.)* We'll give you the money. OK? Are you happy? Howard and I will give you the money and you can keep the store.

MICHAEL. No.

HOWARD. I'm not sure that's the best plan, Holly…

HOLLY. I just want Dad to be happy. That's all I want. If that's our money, then that's our money. I'm not arguing / anymore. This is insane.

SHARON. / Thank you. Thank you, Holly. For saying the one sensible thing anyone has said.

MICHAEL. Except you can't give Dad the money. It's tied up, like Howard said.

HOWARD. That's the problem.

SHARON. So get it untied up. I don't understand that.

HOWARD. It's a lot more complicated than just—there are fees and taxes and just, I would really rather not do that.

SHARON. I would really rather not sell my family history, Howard. Choices, choices.

HOLLY. So we'll pay for now and we can readdress it in a year. I don't care.

HOWARD. A year?

SHARON. Fine.

MICHAEL. No. I need, we can't do that.

HOWARD. I can't guarantee I have the cash for that.

MICHAEL. He doesn't have the cash.

HOLLY. Why not?

MICHAEL. He doesn't have it. He just said that.

HOLLY. That doesn't make a lot of sense to me.

HOWARD. It's tied up / in the stock market and other investments.

HOLLY. / I don't know what that means. I don't understand what that means when you keep saying that.

MICHAEL. *(Losing patience.)* He doesn't have the money, Holly.

HOLLY. What does that mean?

MICHAEL. It's gone. OK? It's gone. That's what it means.

HOWARD. OK. It's / not...

MICHAEL. / Stop. Stop it, Howard. We don't have time for this, I'm sorry. It's gone.

HOLLY. *(To Howard.)* What is he talking about?

    Beat.

What is he talking about, Howard?

HOWARD. It's complicated.

HOLLY. You lost money? What did you do?

HOWARD. It's going to be fine.

MICHAEL. Maybe you should have this conversation / later, Holly.

HOLLY. / What did you do, Howard?

    Beat.

HOWARD. I just...I met someone that needed help.

HOLLY. You *met* someone?

HOWARD. Holly.

HOLLY. Oh my God.

MICHAEL. Take it easy, Holly.

HOLLY. How much money did you give this...person?

HOWARD. We have money.

HOLLY. Then where is it?

HOWARD. Well, a lot of it is just, it's tied up / in, it's tied up.

HOLLY. / If you say tied up one more time, I'm going to tie you up by your fucking balls, Howard. Where is our money?

Pause.

HOWARD. I don't know what you want me to say.

HOLLY. You bastard.

HOWARD. What do you want me to say?

HOLLY. I want you to get the fuck out of this house. That's what I want, Howard.

Pause.

HOWARD. Holly.

HOLLY. Get. The fuck. Out.

Howard stands and exits.
Silence.

SHARON. Look. I'm not giving up my family's, our history, because of whatever kind of creepy thing that Howard did.

HOLLY. Don't, Sharon.

SHARON. I'm not doing it.

MICHAEL. What's the alternative?

SHARON. I guess we'll all just have to pitch in.

ELLEN. We can do that.

MICHAEL. How can we do that?

ELLEN. We can help, Michael. We can obviously, we'll help as much as we can afford to help.

SHARON. Thank you, Ellen.

MICHAEL. We have a mortgage.

ELLEN. So we'll take out another loan. This is family.

SHARON. Thank you.

MICHAEL. We can't take out another loan. Who's going to give us another loan?

ELLEN. We'll figure something out. We always do.

MICHAEL. And what about the two thousand dollars a week for Abby's treatment program? Where do we get that?/ Where does that come from?

99

ELLEN. / That is a temporary expense. She has two more months.

MICHAEL. And then what?

ELLEN. Then she's going back to school in the fall, which we have already set that money aside.

MICHAEL. And how long until they call us from the hospital? How long until the phone rings at three in the morning, because she hasn't / eaten in a week?

ELLEN. / She is doing better.

SHARON. One hundred percent.

ELLEN. She is / working very hard.

MICHAEL. / She's always doing better. She was doing better before Israel. She was doing better *after* Israel.

ELLEN. Well, I happen to have faith in our daughter.

SHARON. I do, too.

MICHAEL. Well, and I see the reality.

ELLEN. And what is the reality?

MICHAEL. The reality? The reality is, our child is sick. She's sick and she's not, she isn't getting better, Ellen. She's not going to get better. We are going to be taking care of Abby for the rest of our lives.

> *Pause.*

I'm sorry. I didn't…

ELLEN. Excuse me.

> *Ellen stands and exits.*

MICHAEL. Ellen.

> *Silence.*

Can we just, let's try maybe to start from the premise that we have no other options here, because, you know, guess what? We have no other options here.

> *Beat.*

SHARON. Why don't we sell the house too?

MICHAEL. Tell us / the alternative.

SHARON. / Why don't we sell the drapes? Fire sale. Let's get rid of it all. Let's make a killing. Maybe we can all retire early.

MICHAEL. What's your better idea, Sharon? We're all waiting to hear it.

SHARON. Dad won't let you do this. You realize that, right? He's not going to let you sell his store.

MICHAEL. He's not in a state of mind to make that decision.

SHARON. According to who?

MICHAEL. According to the fact that it's completely obvious. Look at him. He has no idea what's going on.

SHARON. That's not true.

MICHAEL. Well, then we'll hire a lawyer to prove that it is true.

HOLLY. Oh my God.

SHARON. We are not punishing Dad because you decided to buy an apartment six months before you published *Mein Kampf.*

MICHAEL. OK.

SHARON. Yeah. Maybe if you hadn't felt the need to write a book telling the whole world how much you hate yourself, a book that— by the way—a book that broke your father's heart, OK? Do you think it's a coincidence how sick he is? / Did you think that was just happenstance?

MICHAEL. / OK. You're trying to get me all, you're pushing my buttons and I'm not going to let you, Sharon. Not today.

SHARON. You dragged your family through the dirt. You dragged the six million through dirt, for your own ambition.

MICHAEL. Right. / OK. Right.

SHARON. / So that all of the co-eds on campus, with their Free Palestine T-shirts, would think, oh, what a cool guy he is, he's willing to slander six million dead Jews, what a hero.

MICHAEL. Right.

SHARON. Yeah let's be honest with ourselves, Michael. Let's be honest. You don't believe in anything except for yourself. You're a hypocrite and you're a liar and the fact that your mother begged for you on her deathbed and you were too busy with your *career* to be with her is indicative of a whole lot else wrong with you.

MICHAEL. I was here as soon as I could be.

SHARON. Which was just too fucking late, wasn't it?

MICHAEL. Fuck you, Sharon.

SHARON. Both of you. You made the bed, Holly? You want an award for that? You want a trophy? You vacuumed?

MICHAEL. I think we should vote.

SHARON. You're not selling my store.

MICHAEL. Your store?

SHARON. I'm the only one who cares about it. Who appreciates it.

MICHAEL. You can pretend to be on your high horse about this, Sharon, with your principles and your bullshit, but you and I both know that the only reason you care about any of this is because you're fucking the Guatemalan guy. OK? So save the sanctimony.

HOLLY. What?

MICHAEL. She's sleeping with the guy. Rodrigo. You didn't know this?

SHARON. Thanks for sharing that. Which you swore not to do.

MICHAEL. Oh you're welcome.

HOLLY. Is that true?

MICHAEL. Married man.

SHARON. They're separated now.

MICHAEL. Oh. Well good for you. Great accomplishment. Well done.

SHARON. I'm / pregnant.

MICHAEL. / Fantastic. You've split up a marriage. Give yourself a pat on the back.

HOLLY. You're what? What did you say?

MICHAEL. Your family-values friends in the Republican Party are very impressed.

SHARON. We're having a baby.

Sharon starts to cry.

HOLLY. You're having a baby, Sharon?

Beat.

Sharon?

MICHAEL. I don't believe that.

SHARON. *(Exploding.)* Do you want to look at the fucking sonogram?

Beat.

I'm happy. For the first time in my life, I'm finally…I'm happy.

Beat.
Silence.

MICHAEL. Look. If we don't have this money, then I don't know what else we're going to do. Do you want to put Dad away somewhere? Is that what we want? Do you want to put him in some facility? Some government facility?

Beat.

And now there's a baby? Who's going to take care of the baby, Sharon? How are you going to afford that? Sales from the bargain store? Your teaching salary? How much does that add up to?

Beat.

It's history, I get it. I really, we all want to save history, hold on to our history, I would love to keep the store and pass it on to our children and our grandchildren and, you know, but at what cost? It's a store. It's a parcel of property. It's not some kind of magical place. There are no magical places. There's just dirt. It's all the same dirt. This is our family. The family that is sitting here at this table. The people who came before us, they're not here anymore. There's just us. And Dad is a part of this family. We owe him this. *We* owe *him.*

Michael raises his hand, looks to Holly.

Come on.

Holly raises her hand.

HOLLY. I'm sorry, Sharon.

They look to Sharon.
She begins again to cry, as she slowly raises her hand.
In the living room, Lou struggles to stand and slowly, very slowly he does.
He hobbles slowly, very slowly to the dining room, each step agonizing, precarious.

Dad.

MICHAEL. Dad you should…

SHARON. Let's / go back to your chair, Dad.

103

HOLLY. / Come sit down, Dad.

Lou walks toward Michael.

LOU. No.

He keeps walking closer and closer to Michael.

No.

He looks at all of them.

No no no no no no no no no no no no no—

Black.

Five.

The guest room.
Michael packs his things, not angry anymore, not anything.
In the living room, Lou sits at the table, silent, with Holly,
Sharon, and Ellen.
Joey appears in the door of the guest room.

JOEY. You're leaving?

MICHAEL. Oh. Hi. We are leaving, yes.

JOEY. I didn't really get to see you at all.

MICHAEL. Next time, I guess.

JOEY. When is that going to be?

MICHAEL. I don't know.

JOEY. Maybe Passover.

MICHAEL. Maybe.

Beat.

JOEY. Why was everybody yelling?

MICHAEL. There was just, it was a disagreement.

JOEY. About the store?

Michael nods.

What happened?

MICHAEL. We're, uh, we're selling it. We're going to sell it

JOEY. To who?

MICHAEL. I don't know.

JOEY. When?

MICHAEL. As soon as possible, I guess. I don't…

> *Beat.*

JOEY. I thought we were going to inherit the store. Me and Jennifer and Abby.

MICHAEL. It didn't work out like that.

JOEY. Oh.

> *Beat.*

What are we going to inherit, then?

MICHAEL. I, uh… I really don't know.

> *Beat.*

JOEY. I used to sit up here with Grandma sometimes. When she was sick. It looked like the bed kept getting bigger, and she was just this blue nightgown that got smaller and smaller.

> *Beat.*

MICHAEL. I don't remember that.

> *Beat.*

I didn't…I wasn't here.

> *Beat.*

JOEY. Jews don't believe in Heaven.

MICHAEL. Are you asking me or…?

JOEY. Mom says they don't.

MICHAEL. It's a little more nuanced than that, but…

JOEY. Mom says, the only way people live after they die is if we remember them.

> *Beat.*

Except what happens when all the people who remembered them are dead, too? What happens when the last person who remembers can't remember anymore?

MICHAEL. That's a hard, uh…that's a tough question.

> *Beat.*

JOEY. Is Abby sick now forever?

MICHAEL. Abby is, uh…she's struggling.

JOEY. Can I help her? I would like to help her if I could. She's my cousin. My only cousin.

MICHAEL. I'll let you know if I think of anything.

JOEY. I would like to make sure that she's OK.

MICHAEL. That's very nice.

JOEY. She's my family.

> *Beat.*
> *Michael stands to go.*

MICHAEL. I should probably, uh…

JOEL. What happened to her? In Israel? No one will tell me.

MICHAEL. It's sort of, it's complicated, Joey.

JOEY. I don't mind. I like complicated stuff.

> *Beat.*

Please?

> *Beat.*
> *Michael sits back down.*

MICHAEL. She was, uh, she was in Jerusalem.

JOEY. In Israel?

MICHAEL. Uh. Well. Sort of. It depends on how you…

> *He sees Joey's eyes glaze over.*

She was in Israel, yes. And she was with her group and at some point, we don't really know when, but at some point she decided to leave the group and go on her own.

JOEY. Why?

MICHAEL. Well that's…we don't really know that either. That's when it all gets a little hazy, because she doesn't really remember everything that happened next. Just bits and pieces. She remembers, she climbed up high. And she was looking down at the city. She called us then. I don't know where she was at this point or how she got to a pay phone, but she called us. She said that the city opened up to her. It had opened up, she said, so she could see the insides of it. The earth. All the built-up rock and all the time and the centuries. Ellen didn't, she told her to slow down, but Abby kept going, she couldn't stop. She said: I saw where / Jesus entered on a donkey past the gates of the Old City. I saw where Muhammad came from Mecca…

Lights come up slowly on the living room.

ELLEN. / I saw where Jesus Christ entered on a donkey through the gates of the ancient city. I saw where the Prophet traveled through the night from Mecca on a dream.

MICHAEL. I saw where David laid the foundations of the Temple and I saw / the walls…

HOLLY. / I saw the walls and the altars and the sashes of the priests and I smelled the incense of the burnt offerings.

MICHAEL. I heard the / widows and the orphans.

SHARON. / I heard the wailing and gnashing of teeth of the widows and orphans and strangers.

MICHAEL. I saw the Greeks and the Romans and the Persians and / the Turks.

HOLLY. / I saw the famed warriors of Babylon, the terrible legions of Caesar and Suleiman…

SHARON. Righteous servants all of the One God and the One Faith…

ELLEN. Brandishing cold steel to the throats of the infidels.

MICHAEL. I saw the Crusaders / in their armor.

SHARON. / I saw the Crusaders, sweaty and reverent, burning the bodies of unbelievers in great pyres under the stars.

HOLLY. I saw men in many uniforms, speaking many tongues…

ELLEN. And I saw them all pass away…

HOLLY. One by one…

ELLEN. By one.

SHARON. By one.

HOLLY. Back into the sand from whence they came.

SHARON. I saw kingdoms rise and crumble in a moment…

ELLEN. In a breath.

MICHAEL. I saw the visages of emperors, hard faces stamped on coins of gold and silver, their names long forgotten, lost to time...

SHARON. Vanished back into the sand.

MICHAEL. Everything back into the sand.

As the lights slowly begin to fade.

LOU. Gradually, everything, all of us, everything, in time, swallowed back into the sand.

Dark.

End of Play

PROPERTY LIST

(Use this space to create props lists for your production)

SOUND EFFECTS

(Use this space to create sound effects lists for your production)